MOTHERS OF THE BIBLE

MOTHERS OF THE BIBLE

ANN SPANGLER
JEAN E. SYSWERDA

GRAND RAPIDS, MICHIGAN 49530 USA

ZONDERVAN.COM/
AUTHORTRACKER

We want to hear from you. Please send your comments about this book to us in care of zreview@zondervan.com. Thank you.

ZONDERVAN™

Mothers of the Bible: A Devotional
Copyright © 2006 by Ann Spangler and Jean E. Syswerda

Requests for information should be addressed to:

Zondervan, *Grand Rapids, Michigan 49530*

Library of Congress Cataloging-in-Publication Data

Spangler, Ann.
    Mothers of the Bible / Ann Spangler and Jean E. Syswerda.
        p. cm.
    Adapted from the authors' Women of the Bible.
        ISBN-13: 978-0-310-27239-7 (alk. paper)
        ISBN-10: 0-310-27239-4 (alk. paper)
     1. Mothers in the Bible. 2. Mothers—Religious life. 3.
    Motherhood—Religious aspects—Christianity. I. Syswerda, Jean. II. Title.
    BS579.M65S63 2006
    220.9'20852—dc22
                                                                    2005032792

This edition printed on acid-free paper.

Interior design by Michelle Espinoza

Printed in the United States of America

---

06 07 08 09 10 11 12 • 18 17 16 15 14 13 12 11 10 9 8 7 6 5 4 3 2 1

To Dorothy Eileen Spangler
My favorite mother and friend

To my mom, Gertrude Bloomer,
and my mother-in-law, Lucile Scott Syswerda (1912–2002)
With gratitude for years of love and service

Contents

Introduction

Shortly after Jean Syswerda and I first published *Women of the Bible*, the larger book from which *Mothers of the Bible* is drawn, a publishing colleague confided how astonished he was by the book's immediate success. After encountering it in a local bookstore, he had confidently predicted it would never sell. He smiled as he told me this, glad for our sakes that his prediction had been proved wrong.

I think my colleague made an understandable mistake. He had underestimated the hunger women have for authentic stories about other women who reflect their own struggles to live with faith and hope.

In this book, Jean and I have selected twelve prominent mothers of the Bible, believing that their lives still speak to mothers today. This is true despite the fact that their culture differs vastly from ours. Whether struggling with infertility, the temptation to play favorites among their children, the challenge of single motherhood, or the struggle to believe God's promises regarding their children, these women responded in ways both negative and positive that can help to shape our own experience of God.

In order to help you understand the significance of their stories, we have developed a unique devotional program, combining five different elements: inspiration, background information, Bible study, Bible promises, and prayer. Here's how each of the twelve weeks, focusing on a particular mother of the Bible, unfold:

Monday: Her Story—an inspirational portrait of one mother's life.

Tuesday: Her Life and Times—background information about the culture of her day.

Wednesday: Her Legacy in Scripture—a short Bible study on her life with application to your own.

Thursday: Her Promise—Bible promises that apply to her life and yours.

Friday: Her Legacy of Prayer—praying in light of her story.

By focusing on one mother for five consecutive days, we hope to help you read, reflect, study, and pray in a way that will draw you more deeply into God's presence, helping you to experience his grace as you live out your own call to motherhood.

As in *Women of the Bible*, we suggest beginning with Monday's portrait, designed to help you understand the main elements of the woman's story. After that you may want to read the specific Scriptures that pertain to her life, those mentioned as "Key Scriptures" in the introduction that immediately precedes her story. Though Monday's inspirational retelling at times relies on fictional techniques to bring out various dimensions of a story and the character's emotional responses, every effort has been made to remain close to the original text, drawing out reasonable implications from Scripture's account.

Tuesday will give you an inside look at a particular aspect of the life and culture of the woman whose story is told.

Wednesday is designed to balance Monday's inspirational account by sending you straight to the Bible so you can understand and apply the Scripture to your own life.

Thursday's promises take you a step further, offering Bible verses that can be meditated on, memorized, or copied onto cards that can be placed as reminders at work or at home.

Friday's prayers are designed to build on everything you have already studied and reflected on during the week. By including a balance of praise, thanksgiving, confession, and petition as a basis for your prayer, this section is designed to lead you into deeper communion with God.

Jean and I know that being a mother is one of the most difficult and rewarding challenges in the world. We hope that *Mothers of the Bible* will offer you an opportunity, alone or in a small group, to perceive God's love and faithfulness in fresh ways, blessing your children through the work he does in your life.

We owe special thanks to associate publisher Sandy Vander Zicht for her continuing insight, encouragement, and advocacy for this book, and to senior editor Verlyn Verbrugge for his careful and discerning editing. We are grateful also to creative director Cindy Davis for using her considerable talents to enhance the design of the book and to Zondervan's marketing and sales teams for their sustained efforts to make it available to as many readers as possible.

Eve

Her Name Means *Life-giving* or *Mother of All Who Have Life*

Her Character:	She came into the world perfectly at peace with her God and with her husband, the only other person on the planet. She lived in Paradise, possessing every pleasure imaginable. She never knew the meaning of embarrassment, misunderstanding, hurt, estrangement, envy, bitterness, grief, or guilt until she listened to her enemy and began to doubt God.
Her Sorrow:	That she and her husband were banished from Paradise and the presence of God, and that her first son was a murderer and her second son his victim.
Her Joy:	That she had once tasted Paradise, and that God had promised that her offspring would eventually destroy her enemy.
Key Scriptures:	Genesis 1:26–31; Genesis 2–4

Her Story

The woman stirred and stretched, her skin soft and supple as a newborn's. One finger, then another moved in gentle exploration of the ground that cradled her. She could feel a warmth filling her, tickling her throat as it tried to escape, spilling out in the strong, glad noise of laughter. She felt surrounded, as though by a thousand joys, and then a touch calmed her without diminishing her joy.

Her eyes opened to a Brightness, her ears to a Voice. And then a smaller voice, echoing an elated response: "This is now bone of my bones and flesh of my flesh; she shall be called 'woman,' for she was taken out of man." Adam took hold of her, and their laughter met like streams converging.

The man and the woman walked naked and unashamed in Paradise. No shadows filled Eden — no disorder, discord, or fear.

Then one day a serpent spoke to the woman. "Did God really say, 'You must not eat from any tree in the garden'? You will not surely die. For God knows that when you eat of it your eyes will be opened, and you will be like God, knowing good and evil."

The woman listened. She remembered the Brightness, the Voice of God that had filled her with joy. Could she really be like God? Pressed hard by desire, she took the fruit and then shared it with her husband. Suddenly darkness spread across Eden. It came, not from the outside but from within, filling the man and the woman with shadows, cravings, and misery. Order gave way to disorder, harmony to discord, trust to fear.

Soon Adam and Eve heard the sound of their Creator walking in the garden, and they hid. "Where are you, Adam?" God called.

"I heard you in the garden," Adam replied, "and I was afraid because I was naked; so I hid."

Sin had driven its wedge inside their hearts, and God banished them from Eden, pronouncing judgment first on the wily serpent that had tempted the woman and then on her and on her husband. To the serpent's curse he added this promise: "I will put enmity between you and the woman, and between your offspring and hers; he will crush your head, and you will strike his heel." To the woman, God said: "I will greatly increase your pains in childbearing; with pain you will give birth to children. Your desire will be for your husband, and he will rule over you."

Then God warned Adam that after a lifetime of hard labor, his strength would decrease until his body would finally be wrapped in the dust from which God had formed him. The curse of death fell suddenly upon the new world.

So Adam and his wife were forced to flee Paradise, and Adam named her Eve, because she would be the mother of all the living. But her firstborn, Cain, became a murderer, and her second son, Abel, his victim.

As the years passed, sorrow chased sorrow in the heart of the first woman, and the last we see of her we imagine her not as a creature springing fresh from the hand of God, but as a woman in anguish, giving birth to another child. Her skin now stretches like worn canvas across her limbs, her hands claw the stony ground, grasping for something to hold on to, for anything to ease her pain. She can feel the child inside, filling her, his body pressing for a way of escape. The cries of mother and child meet like streams converging. And Seth is born.

Finally, with her child cradled against her breast, relief begins to spread across Eve's face. With rest her hope returns, a smile forms, and then, finally, laughter rushes from her lips. Try as she might, she cannot stifle her joy. For she remembers the Brightness and the Voice and the promise God gave: Sooner or later, despite many griefs, her seed would crush the serpent. In the end, the woman would win.

Her Life and Times

Childbirth

Eve was the first woman to conceive a child, the first to harbor a fertilized egg in her womb. Did she understand the miracle taking place within her as her belly swelled and her child began to move? Did she know the wonder of love for a child yet unborn? The Bible doesn't give us those answers. But it does tell us that Eve recognized that life was in God's control. At Cain's birth she exclaimed, *"With the help of the LORD I have brought forth a man"* (Genesis 4:1).

God's judgment on Eve — "with pain you will give birth to children" — was no doubt exactly what Eve experienced in birthing this first child. It's the process we appropriately term *labor*. Eve likely bore the pain and went through the entire birth with only Adam's help.

Later, Hebrew women had the help of experienced midwives, who knew remedies for common delivery difficulties. Midwives' responsibilities after the birth included cutting the umbilical cord, washing the newborn, rubbing it with salt for cleansing, and then wrapping it in swaddling cloths.

The birth stool referred to in Exodus 1:16 was probably a low stool on which the mother-to-be squatted, allowing the force of gravity to aid in the birth process. The midwife and possibly other close relatives held the mother's hands to give comfort as well as stability as she bore down.

Women throughout the centuries have borne the results of Eve's sin. Their pain in childbearing unites them in a common bond of an experience shared. The experience is an unusual combination of the earthly and at the same time the unearthly. The pains, the panting, the mess and disorder connected with the birth of a child are of the earth, of Eve herself. But what is brought forth, and the bond between the mother and the child of this experience, is unearthly, something only the Creator of life could forge.

Her Legacy in Scripture

Read Genesis 2:21–23

1. Describe Adam's situation. In this paradise, what need did he have that was not being met that only a woman could fulfill?

Read Genesis 2:24–25

2. What does being "one flesh" in a marriage mean, both physically and spiritually?

3. Think of a couple who truly seems to be "one flesh." What is their relationship like?

Read Genesis 3:1–5

4. This is one of the saddest passages in Scripture, but also the one that sets the stage for all that is to come. How easily do you think the serpent deceived Eve? Do you think she ate of the fruit the first time he approached her, or did he wear her down over a period of time?

Read Genesis 3:6–7

5. What three reasons for eating the fruit are given in verse 6?

6. Eve is rationalizing her sin here. Even though she knows it is wrong, she can come up with a variety of reasons

for eating from the tree anyway. What sorts of reasons do you come up with to rationalize your sin?

Read Genesis 3:8–13

7. Adam and Eve act out a classic scene of passing the blame: Adam blames Eve; Eve blames the serpent. Is any one of the three participants any more or less to blame? What do the curses God pronounces on each tell you about who is "at fault"? (For the serpent, see 3:14–15; for Eve, see 3:16; for Adam, see 3:17–19.)

Read Genesis 3:20–24

8. What is the first thing God does for Adam and Eve after he declares what their punishment will be?

9. Making clothing for Adam and Eve is a practical but also a thoughtful act. What does this tell you about God? What do you think he is willing to do for you after you have sinned and repented?

Read Genesis 4:1–2

10. Whom does Eve acknowledge as the source of life?

THURSDAY

Her Promise

Embedded in the very curse put on Eve for her sin is a wonderful promise. God promises her, and succeeding generations: You "will give birth to children" (Genesis 3:16). God's grace and mercy are marvelously evident, even when he's pronouncing his judgment. He promises that the human race will continue even as he announces that death will now be inevitable.

Throughout Scripture, God's grace is often most beautifully evident within his judgments. When the world was so full of sin that he had to destroy it, God's grace saved Noah and his family. When the Israelites rebelled so thoroughly that captivity was inevitable, God's grace promised restoration. While judgment fell on David for his sin with Bathsheba, God's grace gave them Solomon as a son and successor.

When you are at your lowest, on your knees before God's judgment, never forget that his grace is still at work. And that is truly amazing.

Promises in Scripture

From the fullness of his grace we have all received one blessing after another.
—John 1:16

But where sin increased, grace increased all the more, so that, just as sin reigned in death, so also grace might reign through righteousness to bring eternal life through Jesus Christ our Lord.
—Romans 5:20–21

FRIDAY

Her Legacy of Prayer

So God created human beings in his own image, in the image of God he created them; male and female he created them.

—Genesis 1:27

Reflect On: Genesis 2:15–25; 3.

Praise God: Because he created you in his own image, making you a woman capable of reflecting his love, truth, strength, goodness, wisdom, and beauty.

Offer Thanks: That imbedded in God's judgment of Adam and Eve is the promise of a Redeemer who will crush the head of our enemy, the devil.

Confess: Your own tendency to mar God's image in you by preferring your will to his.

Ask God: To help you surrender your life, so that he can fulfill his purpose for creating you.

Lift Your Heart

Find a peaceful setting, surrounded by the beauty of creation, to meditate on what life must have been like in the garden of Eden. Think about what your life would be like if you experienced peace in all your relationships, if you never suffered physical or emotional pain, if you were never confused or ashamed or guilty, if you always experienced God's love and friendship. Let your imagination run riot as it fills in the details of God's original intention for your life and for those you love.

Then consider this: You were made for paradise. The joys you taste now are infinitesimal compared to those that await you in heaven, for "no eye has seen, no ear has heard, no mind has conceived what God has prepared for those who love him" (1 Corinthians 2:9).

Father, give me a greater understanding of your original plan for our world. Help me to envision its beauty so I might live with a constant awareness that you intend to restore paradise to all who belong to you. May I surrender every sin and every sorrow to you, trusting that you will fulfill your purpose for my life. In Jesus' name I pray, Amen.

Sarah

Her Name Means *Chieftainness* or *Princess*

Her Character:	Beautiful enough to attract rulers in the ancient world, she could be strong-willed and jealous. Yet Sarah was considered a loyal wife who did what was right and who didn't give in to fear.
Her Sorrow:	That she remained childless for most of her life.
Her Joy:	That at the age of ninety, she gave birth to Isaac, child of the promise.
Key Scriptures:	Genesis 12:1 – 20; 16:1 – 8; 17:1 – 22; 18:1 – 15; 21:1 – 13; Galatians 4:22 – 31

Her Story

Sarah was sixty-five, the age many of us retire, when she began a journey that would lead her into uncharted spiritual territory. Leaving behind their homeland, she and her husband, Abraham, moved hundreds of miles south to Canaan, a land fertile with the promises of God but barren of everything cherished and familiar. God had promised the land to Abraham and his offspring. From him would come not just a family, clan, or tribe, but an entire nation, a people who would belong to God as no other people had.

The promise spread like ripples from a stone pitched in water. If Abraham was to father a new nation, surely Sarah would be its mother. Yet she longed to give birth, not to a nation, but to one small child she could kiss and cradle.

At first Abraham and Sarah found it difficult to support themselves, let alone children, in their new homeland. Soon a famine made life so severe that they moved on to Egypt, where Abraham, fearful of Pharaoh, suggested a deceptive maneuver to save his skin: "I know what a beautiful woman you are. When the Egyptians see you, they will say, 'This is his wife.' Then they will kill me but will let you live. Say you are my sister [she was his half sister], so that I will be treated well for your sake and my life will be spared because of you."

So Sarah did as her husband asked, and Pharaoh soon added her to his harem of beautiful women. For the privilege, he paid Abraham in the currency of the day—a bevy of sheep, cattle, donkeys, camels, and servants. But though the two men seemed satisfied with their bargain, God was not. He proceeded to strike Pharaoh and his entire household with diseases. The Egyptian ruler soon summoned Abraham, demanding an explanation. As soon as he heard the truth, he allowed both Sarah and Abraham to leave, taking with them all the riches they had gained in Egypt.

So the couple moved home again. By now, several years had passed since Abraham and Sarah had heard the remarkable promise of God, but still there was no child. So Sarah took matters into her own hands. Following a practice common in the ancient world, she gave Abraham permission to sleep with her Egyptian maid, Hagar. Sarah's slave would become a surrogate mother for the promised child.

Before long, Ishmael was born. But the child brought only discord between the two women.

One day several years later, the Lord appeared to Abraham while he was sitting at the entrance to his tent.

"Where is your wife Sarah?"

"There, in the tent," Abraham replied.

Then the Lord said, "I will surely return to you about this time next year, and Sarah your wife will have a son."

Now Sarah, who had been eavesdropping from inside the tent, laughed and said, "After I am worn out and my master is old, will I now have this pleasure?"

But the Lord said to Abraham, "Why did Sarah laugh and say, 'Will I really have a child, now that I am old?' Is anything too hard for the LORD? I will return to you at the appointed time next year and Sarah will have a son."

Because Sarah was afraid, she lied and said, "I did not laugh."

But the LORD pressed her, saying, "Yes, you did laugh."

A year later, Sarah gave birth to Isaac, whose name means "laughter." Of course the joke was not lost on the ninety-year-old mother, who exclaimed: "God has brought me laughter, and everyone who hears about this will laugh with me."

But Sarah's humor was short-lived. Fireworks flared once again between the two mothers until Sarah forced Hagar and Ishmael from Abraham's household, leaving them to wander in the harsh desert. And though God provided for the two outcasts, it was through Isaac that he would keep his promise of a new nation and a deliverer for his people.

Sarah died at the age of 127 and was buried in Hebron. Between Isaac's birth and her own death lay thirty-seven years, ample time to reflect on her life's adventure with God. Was she ashamed of her treatment of the ill-fated Hagar? Did she remember laughing when God told Abraham she would bear a child at the age of ninety? Did she appreciate the echoing irony in young Isaac's laughter? Did she have any idea she would one day be revered as the Mother of Israel — indeed, a symbol of the promise just as Hagar was to become a symbol of slavery under the law? Scripture does not say. But it is heartening to realize that God accomplishes his purposes despite our frailties, our little faith, our entrenched self-reliance.

True, Sarah's pragmatic attempts to help God keep his promise caused plenty of anguish. (Even in our own day, the struggle between Israel and her Arab neighbors stems from the ancient strife between two women and the children they bore.) Still, despite her jealousy, anxiety, and skepticism about

God's ability to keep his promises, there's no denying that Sarah was a risk-taker of the first order, a woman who said good-bye to everything familiar to travel to a land she knew nothing about. A real flesh-and-blood kind of woman who lived an adventure more strenuous than any fairy-tale heroine, an adventure that began with a promise and ended with laughter.

Her Life and Times

Names

In Bible times, names had a significance they often do not have today. The names that the mothers and fathers of these times gave to their children give us a glimpse into their personal experience, sometimes reflecting their emotional responses to a situation. When Sarah was ninety years old, God told her that she and Abraham would finally have the child for whom she had wished for so long. She could hardly believe it! "After I am worn out and my master is old, will I now have this pleasure?" she exclaimed (Genesis 18:12). When her son was born, Sarah named him Isaac, which means "he laughs," and she said, "God has brought me laughter, and everyone who hears about this will laugh with me" (Genesis 21:6).

Perhaps one of the Bible's most poignant scenes is played out when Rachel, in great pain and knowing she was dying, named her son Ben-Oni, meaning "son of my trouble." But Jacob, the child's father, loving this little one even in his sorrow, renamed him Benjamin, "son of my right hand" (Genesis 35:16–20). When Hannah's son was born, she named him Samuel, which sounds like the Hebrew for "heard of God," because God had heard her cries for a child (1 Samuel 1:20). Many of the Old Testament prophets had names that spoke of their mission: Isaiah's name means "the LORD saves," Obadiah's name means "servant of the LORD," Nahum's name means "comfort," and Malachi's name means "my messenger."

Throughout Scripture, God gives to his people names that offer a picture of their significance and worth to him. We are his "treasured possessions" (Exodus 19:5; Malachi 3:17), the "people of his inheritance" (Deuteronomy 4:20), and "sons of the living God" (Hosea 1:10). We are his "friends" (John 15:15). No matter what your given name, God knows it. In love, he calls you to him by your name, and you belong to him (Isaiah 43:1).

Her Legacy in Scripture

Read Genesis 17:15 – 16

1. *Sarah* means "princess," revealing Sarah's place as a mother of a nation. Do you know the meaning of your name? What significance does its meaning have for you?

2. If you were to ask God to change your name, what would you want your name to be, or to mean?

Read Genesis 18:10 – 15; 21:1 – 7

3. Put yourself in Sarah's position. Do you think you may have laughed also? Why or why not?

4. God fulfilled his promise to Abraham and Sarah in his own time. Describe how you think they felt about God's timing.

5. Have you ever waited for God to fulfill a promise? For what are you waiting right now?

6. As you reflect on the story of Sarah and Abraham, how can you best wait for God to fulfill his promises to you?

Read Genesis 16:6; 18:12, 15; 21:10

7. Choose five adjectives that describe Sarah. In what ways are you similar to Sarah? In what ways are you unlike her?

8. God used Sarah in spite of her failings, her impatience. How can God use you in spite of your imperfections?

Read Genesis 21:1 – 7

9. What did Sarah say when she gave birth to Isaac? Why do you think she said this?
10. Describe a time in your life when God "brought you laughter."

Her Promise

How hard it was for Sarah (and is for us as well) to remember God's promises and to wait for him to fulfill them. God's promises are revealed and fulfilled in his own timing, which is often on a calendar far different from our own.

Waiting patiently for God to work may be one of the most difficult experiences of our Christian walk. We live in an age of the immediate. We think waiting, and doing so *quietly*, is somehow less worthy, perhaps even a bit lazy. We're great "do-it-yourselfers," but we often get in God's way when we take things into our own hands.

Do you have something you're waiting for God to do? Have you asked him for the salvation of your husband? Of a family member? Are you praying for a rebellious child to come home? Whatever the circumstances, God's timing is the best timing. When you're tempted to step in and make things happen on your own, think of Sarah. Her attempts to fulfill God's promise of a son through her servant Hagar had disastrous results. Remember that God has his own timetable, and rest in the assurance that he loves you and will fulfill his promises to you.

Promises in Scripture

> *Wait for the LORD;*
> *be strong and take heart*
> *and wait for the LORD.*

—Psalm 27:14

*I wait for the L*ORD*, my soul waits,*
  and in his word I put my hope.

—Psalm 130:5

*Yet the L*ORD *longs to be gracious to you;*
  he rises to show you compassion.
*For the L*ORD *is a God of justice.*
  Blessed are all who wait for him!

—Isaiah 30:18

*But as for me, I watch in hope for the L*ORD*,*
  I wait for God my Savior;
  my God will hear me.

—Micah 7:7

Her Legacy of Prayer

God also said to Abraham, "As for Sarai your wife, you are no longer to call her Sarai; her name will be Sarah. I will bless her and will surely give you a son by her. I will bless her so that she will be the mother of nations; kings of peoples will come from her."

—Genesis 17:15 – 16

Reflect On: Genesis 17:1 – 22.

Praise God: Because he keeps his promises.

Offer Thanks: That God has a gracious plan for you that will unfold in his time, according to his way.

Confess: Your anxiety and self-reliance.

Ask God: To help you wait with a listening ear and a ready heart to do his will.

Lift Your Heart

God hints at his purpose for you by planting dreams within your heart. Sarah's dream was to give birth to a son. Find a quiet place and spend some time focusing on your dreams. Ask yourself what dreams you've been too busy, too afraid, or too disappointed to pursue. Write them down and pray about each one. God may be telling you to wait, or he may be giving you the go-ahead to pursue one in particular. If it's time to take the plunge, you might just find yourself joyfully echoing Sarah's words in Genesis 21:6: "God has brought me laughter."

Father, thank you for loving me despite the fact that my soul still contains shadows that sometimes block the light of your Spirit. As I grow older, may I trust you more completely for the dreams you've implanted in my soul, the promises you've made to me. Like Sarah, may I be surrounded by laughter at the wonderful way you accomplish your purpose despite my weakness. In Jesus' name, Amen.

Hagar

Her Name (Egyptian) May Mean *Fugitive* or *Immigrant*

Her Character: A foreigner and slave, she let pride overtake her when she became Abraham's wife. A lonely woman with few resources, she suffered harsh punishment for her mistake. She obeyed God's voice as soon as she heard it and was given a promise that her son would become the father of a great nation.

Her Sorrow: That she was taken from her homeland to become a slave in a foreign land, where she was mistreated for many years.

Her Joy: To know that God cared, that he saw her suffering and heard her cry, and that he helped her when she needed him most.

Key Scriptures: Genesis 16; 21:8 – 21; Galatians 4:22 – 31

Her Story

An Egyptian slave and Sarah's bitter rival, Hagar still had one thing going for her that her mistress never enjoyed: a personal revelation of God, who lovingly intervened on her behalf, not once but twice. It happened when she was alone and afraid, without a shekel to her name — but that's getting ahead of the story.

You may remember that Abraham, whom we honor as the father of faith, showed little evidence of that faith when he and Sarah first entered Egypt to escape a famine in Canaan. Certain the Egyptians would kill him once they caught sight of his beautiful wife, he advised her to pose as his sister. Soon enough, Pharaoh added Sarah to his harem and rewarded Abraham with an abundance of camels, sheep, cattle, donkeys, and servants. But God punished Pharaoh for his unwitting error so effectively that, when he found out that Sarah was actually Abraham's wife, he ordered the two of them to leave Egypt with all their belongings. Possibly, Hagar was part of the booty Abraham and Sarah took with them — a gift they later regretted.

Still, of the three parties involved in the scheme to make Hagar a surrogate mother, she was perhaps the only innocent one, a slave with little power to resist. When Sarah told Abraham to sleep with her maid, she opened the door to spiritual catastrophe. As soon as Hagar discovered her pregnancy, she began lording it over her mistress, hardly a smart move for a young foreigner up against a woman entrenched in her husband's affections.

In fact, Sarah made life so difficult for Hagar that she fled into the desert, a desperate move for a pregnant woman who was so far from home.

She hadn't gotten far before she heard a voice calling, "Hagar, servant of Sarai, where have you come from, and where are you going? Go back to your mistress and submit to her." But then, as if to sweeten the order, came a word of assurance: "You will have a son. You shall name him Ishmael, for the LORD has heard of your misery."

Remarkably, Hagar didn't argue but returned to Abraham and Sarah. Like a stream of water in the desert, God's word had penetrated the wilderness of her heart. Her bondage, her bitterness, her anxiety about the future—God had seen every bit of it. He knew about the child in her womb, naming him Ishmael, meaning "God hears." In the years to come, whenever Hagar would hold her son close, watch him play, or worry about his future, she would remember that God was near, listening for the child's cry. Little wonder that she had responded to the voice in the desert by calling the Lord "the God who sees me."

Some sixteen years later, Hagar found herself once again in the wilderness, this time by force rather than by choice. In a crescendo of bitterness against her younger rival, Sarah had expelled Hagar and Ishmael from their home. Dying from thirst, Hagar placed her son under a bush and withdrew, unable to witness his agony.

Her weeping was soon broken by an angel's voice, "Do not be afraid; God has heard the boy crying as he lies there.

Lift the boy up and take him by the hand, for I will make him into a great nation." With that, the angel of the Lord opened Hagar's eyes so that she discovered a well of water nearby that would save her son's life. (The well became known as *Beer Lahai Roi*, or the "well of the Living One who sees me.")

The last we see of Hagar, she is living in the Desert of Paran in the Sinai Peninsula, busy securing a wife, and therefore a future, for Ishmael. God had made a way in the wilderness for a single woman and her son, without friends, family, or resources to help her. He had seen, he had heard, and he had indeed been faithful.

Her Life and Times

Slavery and Surrogate Motherhood

Slavery was common practice in ancient Eastern culture, so common that God's laws made provision for its safe and fair practice but not for its destruction. Slaves were obtained in any of a number of ways: captives from war became slaves, particularly virgin women (Numbers 31:7–32); men and women and their children went into slavery to pay debts (Leviticus 25:39); slaves could be purchased (Leviticus 25:44); and sometimes slavery was even voluntary, as when a male slave who could have gone free remained in servitude in order to stay with a wife he loved (Exodus 21:2–6).

Hagar, an Egyptian, probably became a slave to Abraham and Sarah when they left Egypt (Genesis 12:20). Leaving her homeland behind, she made herself useful and proved herself trustworthy, thereby becoming Sarah's maidservant, a position of some importance in the household.

Sarah must have had some confidence and perhaps even affection for Hagar to want her to be the surrogate mother of her son. Such practices were fairly common in that day. Infertile women urged their husbands to take their maidservants in order to gain a child and heir for the family. Female slaves were often made the concubines or wives of the master or one of his sons. Their children became the property and sometimes the heirs of their masters. As female slaves, they had no choice in the matter. They were alone, with no rights and no one to defend them.

Many women today are in a position similar to Hagar's. They may not be actual slaves, but they are in positions of weakness, with no one to defend them. No one except God. The same God who defended Hagar and heard the cries of her son in the desert hears the cries of helpless women and their children today. When we are at our weakest, God is at his best, ready to step in and say to us as he said to Hagar, "Do not be afraid" (Genesis 21:17).

Her Legacy in Scripture

Read Genesis 16:1–4a

1. Sarah's proposition was a customary one of that day. Hagar had little say in the matter, but she must have had some reaction to it. What do you think Hagar's reaction might have been?

2. What sort of reaction do you have when you find yourself in a position over which you have no control? How can God help you when you are in such a position?

Read Genesis 16:4b–5

3. Why do you think the pregnant Hagar began to despise Sarah?

Read Genesis 16:6–8

4. The area to which Hagar ran away was probably pretty barren and sparsely populated. Describe how desperate she must have been to run away from a difficult but safe situation to the "desert."

5. Have you ever been that desperate? What were the circumstances?

Read Genesis 16:9–12

6. God's words to Hagar here are words of assurance but also of prophecy. Her descendants would be "too

numerous to count," but the son through whom those descendants would come would "be a wild donkey of a man." What picture of Ishmael does that put into your mind? What kind of a man do you think he was?

7. Do you have family members who, like Ishmael, "live in hostility"? How do you respond to them? What can you do to improve your relationship with them?

Read Genesis 21:8 – 21

8. Even though Hagar and Ishmael were outcasts and alone, God lovingly cared for them. Describe how you think Hagar felt when she laid Ishmael down and went away because she "could not watch the boy die." How did God meet her needs?

9. In what ways has God met your needs when you were despairing and alone?

10. Are you in a desperate situation right now? Read Genesis 21:19 again. Might there be a "well" to which you can go for sustenance, if only you could see it? Ask God to open your eyes to the way out of your situation just as he opened Hagar's eyes and aided her in her desperation.

THURSDAY

Her Promise

A thin young woman sits huddled in the front seat of her car. She covers her ears to block out the sound of her little son as he whimpers with cold in the backseat. Her husband abandoned her and the boy two months before. Left without resources, she was soon turned out of her apartment. The car is now their only home. It has long since seen its last drop of gasoline, and its worn interior provides little protection from the winter winds outside.

This modern-day Hagar is no further from God's promises than was Hagar herself as she poured out her sorrow in the desert. God sees her heartache, just as he saw Hagar's. Though you may not be as desperate as Hagar or her modern counterpart, you may have experienced times in your life that made you fear for the future. Whether you are living in a wilderness of poverty or loneliness or sorrow, God's promises, love, and protection are just as available to you now as they were to Hagar.

Promises in Scripture

> *I will lie down and sleep in peace,*
> *for you alone, O LORD,*
> *make me dwell in safety.*

—Psalm 4:8

My comfort in my suffering is this:
  Your promise preserves my life.

—Psalm 119:50

Though I walk in the midst of trouble,
  you preserve my life;
you stretch out your hand against the anger of my foes,
  with your right hand you save me.

—Psalm 138:7

Her Legacy of Prayer

"What is the matter, Hagar? Do not be afraid; God has heard the boy crying as he lies there. Lift the boy up and take him by the hand, for I will make him into a great nation."

—Genesis 21:17–18

Reflect On: Genesis 21:8–21.

Praise God: Because he is an all-knowing Father who hears the cries of his children. Nothing that happens to us can ever escape his notice.

Offer Thanks: That the Lord runs after the weak and the helpless, to show them his mercy and his plan of blessing for their lives.

Confess: Any pride, selfishness, or other sin that may have contributed to difficulties in your life.

Ask God: To open your eyes to the way he is protecting and providing for you and your children. Ask him to help you live each day, not as a slave to the law but as a child of grace.

Lift Your Heart

Invite a couple of close friends to share a Middle Eastern feast with olives, figs, pita bread, nuts, hummus, tabbouleh, and your favorite drink. Pray a special grace thanking God for providing so richly for you even when you felt you were living through a desert season in your life. Share stories with each other about how God has provided even when you weren't sure he was listening to your prayers.

Hummus

In a food processor blend 2 cups of cooked or canned chickpeas, drained, with 2/3 cup sesame paste (tahini), 3/4 cup lemon juice, salt and freshly ground pepper to taste, and 2 peeled garlic cloves. Stir in 1/4 cup finely chopped scallions. Makes about 3 cups. A great dip for bread, chips, or fresh vegetables.

Tabbouleh

1. Place 3/4 cup uncooked cracked wheat in a glass bowl and cover with cold water for 30 minutes; then drain completely. (For a softer texture, cover with boiling water and let stand for one hour before draining.)
2. Add 1 1/2 cups chopped fresh parsley; 3 medium tomatoes, chopped; 5 green onions, thinly sliced (with tops); and 2 tablespoons chopped fresh or 2 teaspoons crushed dried mint leaves.
3. In a separate bowl, mix 1/4 cup olive oil, 1/4 cup lemon juice, 3/4 teaspoon salt, and 1/4 teaspoon pepper. Pour over cracked wheat mixture and toss.
4. Cover and refrigerate at least one hour. Serve with a garnish of mint leaf. Makes 6 servings, about 3/4 cup each.

Lord, sometimes I feel abandoned, as though no one understands or cares about me. Please show me that you really are near and that you see and hear everything that happens. Refresh me with your presence even when I am walking through a desert experience. And help me, in turn, to comfort others when they feel hopeless and alone.

Rebekah

Her Name Probably Means *Loop* or *Tie*

Her Character: Hard-working and generous, her faith was so great that she left her home forever to marry a man she had never seen or met. Yet she played favorites with her sons and failed to trust God fully for the promise he had made.

Her Sorrow: That she was barren for the first twenty years of her married life, and that she never again set eyes on her favorite son, Jacob, after he fled from his brother Esau.

Her Joy: That God had gone to extraordinary lengths to pursue her, to invite her to become part of his people and his promises.

Key Scriptures: Genesis 24; 25:19 – 34; 26:1 – 28:9

Her Story

The sun was dipping beyond the western rim of the sky as the young woman approached the well outside the town of Nahor, five hundred miles northeast of Canaan. It was women's work to fetch fresh water each evening, and Rebekah hoisted the brimming jug to her shoulder, welcoming its cooling touch against her skin.

As she turned to go, a stranger greeted her, asking for a drink. Obligingly, she offered to draw water for his camels as well. Rebekah noticed the look of surprised pleasure that flashed across his face. Ten camels could put away a lot of water, she knew. But had she overheard his whispered prayer just moments earlier, her astonishment would have exceeded his. The man had prayed, "O LORD, God of my master Abraham, give me success today, and show kindness to my master Abraham. May it be that when I say to a girl, 'Please let down your jar that I may have a drink,' and she says, 'Drink, and I'll water your camels too' — let her be the one you have chosen for your servant Isaac."

A simple gesture. A generous response. A young woman's future altered in a moment's time. The man Rebekah encountered at the well, Abraham's servant, had embarked on a sacred mission — to find Isaac a wife from among Abraham's own people rather than from among the surrounding Canaanites. Like her great-aunt Sarah before her, Rebekah would make the journey south to embrace a future she could hardly glimpse. Betrothed to a man twice her age, whose name meant "laughter," she felt a sudden giddiness rise inside her. The God of Abraham and Sarah was wooing her, calling her name and no other, offering a share in the promise. God was forging a new nation to be his own people.

Isaac was forty when he first set eyes on Rebekah. Perhaps his heart echoed the joy of that first man, "Here at last is bone of my bones and flesh of my flesh!" So Isaac and Rebekah entered the tent of his mother Sarah and made love. And the Bible says that Rebekah comforted Isaac after the death of his mother.

Rebekah was beautiful and strong like Sarah, yet she bore no children for the first twenty years of her life with Isaac. Would she suffer as Sarah did the curse of barrenness? Isaac prayed and God heard, giving her not one, but two sons, who wrestled inside her womb. And God told her: "Two nations are in your womb, and two peoples from within you will be separated; one people will be stronger than the other, and the older will serve the younger."

During the delivery, Jacob grasped the heel of his brother Esau, as though striving for first position. Though second by birth, he was first in his mother's affections. But his father loved Esau best.

Years later, when Isaac was old and nearly blind, he summoned his firstborn, Esau. "Take your quiver and bow and hunt some wild game for me. Prepare the kind of meal I like, and I will give you my blessing before I die."

But the clever Rebekah overheard and called quickly to Jacob, suggesting a scheme to trick the blessing from Isaac.

Disguised as Esau, Jacob presented himself to his father for the much-coveted blessing.

Isaac then blessed Jacob, thinking he was blessing Esau: "May nations serve you and peoples bow down to you. Be lord over your brothers, and may the sons of your mother bow down to you. May those who curse you be cursed and those who bless you be blessed."

Isaac had stretched out his hand and passed the choicest blessing to his younger son, thus recalling the words spoken about the two children jostling for position in Rebekah's womb. The benediction thus given could not be withdrawn, despite the deceit, despite Esau's tears, and despite his vow to kill Jacob.

Afraid lest Esau take revenge, Rebekah persuaded Isaac to send Jacob north to find a wife from among her brother Laban's daughters.

As the years passed, Rebekah must have longed to embrace her younger son, hoping for the privilege of enfolding his children in her embrace. But more than twenty years would pass before Jacob returned. And though Isaac would live to welcome his son, Rebekah would not.

When Rebekah was a young girl, God had invited her to play a vital role in the story of his people. He had gone to great lengths to pursue her. Like Sarah, she would become a matriarch of God's people, and like Sarah, her heart would divide itself between faith and doubt, believing that God's promise required her intervention. Finding it difficult to rest in the promise God had made, she resorted to trickery to achieve it.

The results, mirroring her own heart, were mixed. Though Jacob indeed became heir to the promise, he was driven from his home and the mother who loved him too well. In addition, he and his descendants would forever be at odds with Esau and his people, the Edomites. Two thousand years later, Herod the Great, who hailed from Idumea (the Greek and Roman name for Edom) would slaughter many innocent children in his attempt to destroy the infant Jesus.

Yet God was still at work, graciously using a woman whose response to him was far less than perfect, in order to accomplish his purposes.

Her Life and Times

Jewelry

"Then I put the ring in her nose and the bracelets on her arms." … Then the servant brought out gold and silver jewelry and articles of clothing and gave them to Rebekah.

— Genesis 24:47, 53

A nose ring! Often taken as a sign of rebellious youth today, a nose ring was an acceptable form of adornment in ancient times. When Abraham's servant realized Rebekah was the woman Isaac was to marry, he immediately got out the jewels he had brought along for the occasion. He gave her two gold bracelets and a gold nose ring. Rebekah quickly slipped the jewelry on and ran home with shining eyes to tell her family what had occurred.

A nose ring is mentioned only two other times in Scripture — in Proverbs 11 and Ezekiel 16. In Ezekiel 16, God is describing in allegorical terms how much he loves the city of Jerusalem. He lovingly bathes her, then dresses her in wonderfully rich clothing and soft leather sandals. He then tenderly adorns her with jewelry. "I put bracelets on your arms and a necklace around your neck, and I put a ring on your nose, earrings on your ears and a beautiful crown on your head. So you were adorned with gold and silver" (Ezekiel 16:11 – 13).

The Old Testament mentions jewels and jewelry numerous times. Women and men both wore earrings (Exodus 32:2). They also commonly wore "armlets, bracelets, signet rings, earrings and necklaces" (Numbers 31:50). The Israelites took most of their jewelry from others while at war; gold and silver and gemstones are often listed among the booty taken during a raid. According to 2 Samuel 8:11, David gained enormous amounts of gold and silver and bronze when he conquered the nations surrounding Israel. He dedicated all of it to the Lord, and his son Solomon used it to build the fabulous temple in Jerusalem. Believe it or not, Solomon had so much gold in his kingdom that he "made silver and gold as common in Jerusalem as stones" (2 Chronicles 1:15).

In the NIV, the Greek word for various female adornments is translated "jewelry" only once. In speaking to wives, Peter urges them to pay more attention to their inner beauty than their outward beauty. "Your beauty should not come from outward adornment, such as braided hair and the wearing of gold jewelry and fine clothes," he says. "Instead, it should be that of your inner self, the unfading beauty of a gentle and quiet spirit, which is of great worth in God's sight" (1 Peter 3:3–4). Evidently, the women of New Testament times were as fascinated with jewelry as the women of Old Testament times — and the women of our times. How easy and common it is to look in the mirror to assess our outward appearance, but how seldom do most of us spend as much or more time examining our inner appearance!

Tomorrow morning, when you put your rings on your fingers, also put on a spirit of peace. When you put your earrings on your ears, put them on with a cheerful attitude. When you clasp your necklace around your neck, clasp a sweet spirit to your heart also. The jewelry you wear won't make much difference in your day, but the spirit you wear will.

Her Legacy in Scripture

Read Genesis 24:15 – 27

1. What does this first information about young Rebekah tell you about her looks and her character?

2. How are you like Rebekah? How are you different from her?

Read Genesis 24:28 – 50

3. In these verses Abraham's servant tells Rebekah's family how he met her, emphasizing the Lord's blessing and involvement throughout. How does Rebekah's family respond?

Read Genesis 24:51 – 58

4. Three simple words in verse 58 changed Rebekah's life forever. Who was she like in her willingness to go where she had never been before?

5. How would you react if God called you away from home and family? What would have to happen to make you obey?

Read Genesis 24:67

6. These are some of the sweetest words about marriage found in the Bible. In your own words, describe what you think Isaac and Rebekah's marriage was like in these early days.

Read Genesis 25:28

7. These are some of the saddest words about parenting found in the Bible. Describe how you think the favoritism of Isaac and Rebekah affected Jacob and Esau and their relationship.

8. Many children grow up thinking their parents are favoring one sibling or another. If you have children, how can you avoid such thinking in them?

Read Genesis 27:1 – 28:9

9. Why do you think Rebekah resorts to trickery to gain the promise given to her when she was pregnant?

10. Describe how you think Rebekah may have felt ten years later. Do you think she regretted her actions?

11. How are Rebekah's actions like those of her mother-in-law Sarah?

12. The story of Rebekah is rich and colorful. In one sentence summarize what you would like to learn from her life.

Her Promise

Rebekah heard Abraham's servant describe how he had prayed and how he was sure she was the woman God intended for Isaac. God himself had divinely orchestrated the events. Rebekah seemed to have known that, and when asked she answered simply, "I will go."

Did Rebekah fully realize God's plan for her? Was she open to following that plan? Or was she simply entranced with the romantic notions of a young girl looking for her knight in shining armor? Whatever her motivation, the events *were* planned by God, and he was able and willing to faithfully continue to fulfill his promises through her.

God's faithfulness, despite our waywardness and contrariness, is evident both throughout Scripture and throughout our lives. He will be faithful; he promises.

Promises in Scripture

> *Know therefore that the LORD your God is God; he is the faithful God, keeping his covenant of love to a thousand generations of those who love him and keep his commands.*

—Deuteronomy 7:9

> *The LORD is faithful to all his promises*
> *and loving toward all he has made.*

—Psalm 145:13

Let us hold unswervingly to the hope we profess, for he who promised is faithful.

—Hebrews 10:23

Her Legacy of Prayer

"Our sister, may you increase to thousands upon thousands; may your offspring possess the gates of their enemies."

—Genesis 24:60

Reflect On: Genesis 27.

Praise God: Because unlike Isaac, who had only one blessing to give his children, God has blessings uniquely designed for each of us.

Offer Thanks: That God doesn't wait until we are perfect to involve us in his plans.

Confess: Your tendency to try to control the future, rather than trusting God to shape it according to his timetable.

Ask God: To protect you from playing favorites with your own children and to trust that he has a generous plan for each one.

Lift Your Heart

Take a few minutes this week to write a blessing card for each of your children. Use a simple index card or decorate the card with stickers, stencils, or line drawings. (If you don't have children of your own, you can do this for a niece or nephew or another special child in your life.)

Start by praying for each child, asking God's blessing on their lives. Then write out the blessings you sense God wants for them. Tuck the blessing cards under their pillows or place them next to their dinner plates. Tell them these are some of the ways you are asking God to bless them. Be sure to keep a copy of each card for yourself so you can make those blessings a subject of frequent prayer.

Lord, you give us the power to bless our children, through our example, our teaching, our love, and our prayers. May our children surpass us in faith. In all their struggles may they sense your nearness, and may their joy be renewed each morning. May each of them become the kind of person that attracts others to you. I pray this in the name of Jesus, Amen.

Rachel

Her Name Means *Ewe*

Her Character: Manipulated by her father, she had little say over her own life circumstances and relationships. But rather than dealing creatively with a difficult situation, Rachel behaved like a perpetual victim, responding to sin with yet more sin, making things worse by competing with her sister and deceiving her father in return.

Her Tragedy: That her longing for children ultimately led to her death in childbirth.

Her Joy: That her husband cherished her and would do whatever was in his power to make her happy.

Key Scriptures: Genesis 29–35; Jeremiah 31:15; Matthew 2:18

Her Story

Was it better to have love with no children or to be unloved and yet be mother to a house full of sons? The question battered Rachel like a strong wind slamming the same door over and over.

Leah had just given birth to her fourth son, Judah. In her joy she had shouted, "I will praise the LORD!" Her firstborn, Reuben, meant "see, a son," Simeon, "one who hears," and Levi, "attached," as though Jacob could ever be attached to his plain wife! Rachel was sick to death of this habit her sister had of naming her sons in ways that emphasized Rachel's own barrenness.

Leah had become Jacob's wife through her father's treachery, but Rachel had captured his love from their first meeting at the well outside Haran. Every touch communicated his favor. Yet favor could not make children any more than wishing could make riches. Rachel should have been his first, his only wife, just as Aunt Rebekah was Uncle Isaac's only wife.

Rachel's father, Laban, had promised her to his nephew, Jacob, provided he work for him for seven years. Seven years was a long time to wait for a wife, yet Jacob had thought it a good bargain. And that made Rachel love him all the more.

But as the wedding day approached, Laban hatched a scheme to trick seven more years of labor out of Jacob. Rachel's day of happiness dissolved the moment Laban instructed her older sister, Leah, to disguise herself in Rachel's wedding garments.

After dark he led Leah, veiled, to Jacob's tent, and the two slept together as man and wife. As the first light crept across the tent floor, Jacob reached again for Rachel only to find Leah at his side. Laban's treachery stung him. It was beyond belief. Even so, despite the recriminations and the tears, the marriage could not be undone.

But Rachel felt undone, her blessing seized by stealth. Laban's convoluted plan, however, was still unfolding. He struck another bargain, giving Rachel to Jacob the very next week in exchange for seven more years of labor. So now the two sisters lived uneasily together, Leah's sons a grating reminder that Rachel, the second wife, was cheated still.

"Give me children, or I'll die," Rachel screamed at Jacob one day—as though he could take the place of God and open her womb. So she gave him Bilhah, her maid, who conceived and bore her two sons. When Napthali, the second son, was born, Rachel proclaimed to anyone who would listen, "I have had a great struggle with my sister, and I have won." But the wrestling match between Rachel and Leah was far from over.

Rachel's bitterness again eased when she herself gave birth to a son, naming him Joseph, meaning "may he add"—a prophetic prayer that God would add yet another child to her line.

Then one day God spoke to Jacob, telling him to return to the land of Isaac, his father. More than twenty years earlier, Jacob had wrestled the blessing from Esau and then had fled his murderous wrath. Had the long years paid him back twofold? Had Laban's treachery and the wrestling match between Rachel and Leah reminded him of his own struggles with his brother? Would God — and Esau — call it even? Only the Lord could protect him in this matter with his brother.

As Jacob gathered his flocks, his servants, and his children, preparing to leave, Rachel stole her father's household gods, small idols thought to ensure prosperity. After ten days on the road, Laban overtook them in the hill country of Gilead, accusing his son-in-law of theft. Unaware of Rachel's deceit, Jacob invited Laban to search the camp, promising to put to death anyone discovered with the idols.

Having learned a trick or two from her crafty father, Rachel tucked the idols into a saddle and then sat on it. When Laban entered her tent, she greeted him with a woman's ruse, saying, "Don't be angry, my lord, that I cannot stand up in your presence; I'm having my period." Her trick worked, much as Jacob's had when he deceived his own father, and Laban finally gave up the search. Later, Jacob made sure that all the old idols were purged from his household.

As they made their way across the desert, Jacob faced his brother Esau, and the two reconciled. But tragedy soon overtook them as Rachel struggled to give birth to a second son, the answer to her many prayers. Ironically, the woman who once said she would die unless she had children was now dying in childbirth. Rachel's last words, "He is Ben-Oni, the son of my trouble," capture her anguish at the birth of this son.

But Jacob gathered the infant in his arms and with a father's tenderness renamed him Benjamin, "son of my right hand."

Like her husband, the beautiful Rachel had been both a schemer and the victim of schemes. Tricked by her own father, she viewed her children as weapons in the struggle with her sister. As so often happens, the lessons of treachery and competition were passed from generation to generation. Rachel's own son, Joseph, would suffer grievously as a result, being sold into slavery by his half brothers, Leah's sons.

Yet God would remain faithful. Through a remarkable set of twists and turns, Rachel's Joseph would one day rule Egypt, providing a refuge for his father and brothers in the midst of famine. Step by step, in ways impossible to foresee, God's plan was unfolding—a plan to heal divisions, put an end to striving, and restore hope. Using people with mixed motives and confused desires (the only kind of people there are), he was revealing his grace and mercy, never once forsaking his promise.

Her Life and Times

Menstrual Cycles

"Rachel said to her father, 'Don't be angry, my lord, that I cannot stand up in your presence; I'm having my period.' So [Laban] searched but could not find the household gods" (Genesis 31:35). Rachel's words here are the only mention in Scripture of a typical monthly menstrual cycle, other than the ceremonial laws covering menstruation found in Leviticus and referred to again in Ezekiel.

Rachel knew without a doubt that her ploy would successfully deter her father. By claiming to have her period, she not only kept the false gods she had stolen, she kept her very life, since Jacob had promised to kill whoever had stolen the idols from Laban.

During the time a Hebrew woman had her period, she was considered "unclean," not really surprising considering the untidy nature of a monthly flow, especially in these days, long before the invention of feminine sanitary products. But the laws were more stringent than just to cover the very personal nature of a monthly period. Those who touched a woman at this time, even by chance, became unclean until evening. Wherever the woman slept or sat also became unclean. Anyone who touched her bedding or her seat was considered unclean until they washed their clothes, bathed, and waited until evening.

A woman was considered unclean for seven days, the normal length of a woman's monthly period. She then customarily bathed in order to cleanse herself. This is probably the bath that Bathsheba was taking when spotted by King David (2 Samuel 11:2–4). Since she had just had her period, David could be sure Bathsheba's child was his when she told him she was pregnant (her husband was a soldier off to war).

The natural flow of a woman's period didn't require sacrifices for her to be cleansed; merely bathing and waiting for a prescribed time was enough. A longer, less natural flow, usually caused by some infection or disease, required a sacrifice in order for the woman to be clean. Neither implied any moral failing on the part of the woman, but since blood was seen as a source of life, anything surrounding it became an important part of ceremonial law.

Many women consider their monthly period, and the discomfort and irritability that often come along with it, a monthly trial—something women must bear, and men, lucky creatures, are spared. However, it is only through this particular function of her body that a woman can reproduce and carry a child. Although at times messy, at times a nuisance, at times downright painful, only through this process does a woman have the opportunity afforded to no man—the opportunity to bear new life. And in so doing, to be uniquely linked to the Creator of all life.

Her Legacy in Scripture

Read Genesis 29:30

1. How do you think most women would respond to the situation in which Rachel found herself? With love and concern for her unloved sister? Or with a spirit of superiority and pride?

Read Genesis 30:1

2. The agony expressed by Rachel's words here is an agony experienced by many women over the centuries. How did Rachel's close relationship with Leah increase her pain? Is there any way their relationship could have eased her pain instead?

Compare Genesis 29:30–31 and 30:1

3. These two sisters each had something the other wanted. What did Rachel have that Leah wanted? What did Leah have that Rachel wanted?

4. Discontentment is an insidious thing, trapping us into thinking that which was enough is no longer enough, and that which was satisfying is no longer satisfying. Do you ever feel discontent because you don't "have it all"? What can you do to resist such sentiments?

Read Genesis 31:19, 30–34

5. Why would Rachel even have such idols? Why do you think she hid them from her father?

6. When have you been in a situation that caused you to lie or cheat to protect yourself or someone else? Describe it. What could/should you have done differently?

Read Genesis 35:16 – 20

7. Given the fact that they were on a journey, describe in your own words the situation under which Rachel likely gave birth.

8. It's one of the paradoxes of life, revealed here in this tragic story of Rachel's death, that what we most want from life we often can only gain by giving up something else that's equally important to us. Can you think of an instance in your own life in which gaining something you wanted required giving up something else?

9. Jacob renamed his new son Benjamin, which means "son of my right hand." What does this new name reveal about Jacob's hope for the future?

Her Promise

Genesis 30:22 says "God remembered Rachel; he listened to her and opened her womb." God *remembered* Rachel, but he had never really forgotten her. When the Bible uses the word *remember*, it doesn't mean that God forgets and then suddenly recalls—as if the all-knowing, all-powerful God of the universe suddenly hits his forehead with the heel of his hand and says, "Oops! I forgot all about Rachel. I'd better do something quickly!"

No, when the Bible says God remembers something, it expresses God's love and compassion for his people. It reminds us of God's promise never to abandon us or leave us without support or relief. He will never forsake us. He will never forget us. He will always *remember* us.

Promises in Scripture

Then God remembered Rachel; he listened to her and opened her womb.

—Genesis 30:22

Remember, O LORD, your great mercy and love,
for they are from of old.

—Psalm 25:6

You understand, O LORD;
remember me and care for me.

—Jeremiah 15:15

The Mighty One has done great things for me—holy is his name.

—Luke 1:49

Her Legacy of Prayer

Then God remembered Rachel; he listened to her and opened her womb.

—Genesis 30:22

Reflect On: Genesis 30:1–24.

Praise God: Because he never for a moment forgets about us. He is present and attentive, aware of our deepest desires, even when we're certain he's lost track of us.

Offer Thanks: That God alone is the Creator. Because of him, every human life is sacred.

Confess: That we sometimes use our children, our husbands, our homes, or even the size of our paychecks to compete with other women.

Ask God: To help you form deep and loyal friendships with other women so you can know the joy that comes from being sisters in Christ.

Lift Your Heart

Think of one woman you would like to get to know better in the next few months. Then pick up the phone and make a lunch date, or invite her to a play, movie, or concert. Make sure you build in a little time to chat so you can begin to build a relationship. One expert says it takes an average of three years to form a solid friendship. Don't waste another moment!

Father, forgive me for letting my identity rest on whose wife or mother I am or what kind of job I have. I don't want to view other women as my rivals but as potential friends and even soul mates. Please lead me to the friendships I desire, and help me to be patient with the process. Amen.

Leah

Her Name May Mean *Impatient* or *Wild Cow*

Her Character: Capable of both strong and enduring love, she was a faithful mother and wife. Manipulated by her father, she became jealous of her sister, with whom, it seems, she never reconciled.

Her Sorrow: That she lacked her sister's beauty, and that her love for her husband was one-sided.

Her Joy: That she bore Jacob six sons and one daughter.

Key Scriptures: Genesis 29 – 35; Ruth 4:11

Her Story

We buried my sister Rachel today. But she is still alive. I catch glimpses of her in Jacob's broken heart, in dark-eyed Joseph and squalling little Benjamin, his favorite sons. Rachel's sons. I can hear my beautiful, determined sister weeping loudly for the children she might have had, stubbornly refusing to be comforted. Yet who takes note of my tears? Should they flood the desert, no one would notice.

Reuben, Simeon, Levi, Judah, Issachar, Zebulun, Dinah, and then Gad and Asher by my maid—these are the children God has given me and I have given my beloved Jacob. And still he loves her best. Should my husband and I live another hundred years, I will never be his only wife.

                         ◦⌒◯⌒◦

Contrary to what Leah may have felt, God *had* taken note of her sorrow. Knowing well that Jacob's heart was too cramped a space to harbor both Rachel and Leah, he made Leah a mother, not once, but seven times, extending her influence in Jacob's household.

With the birth of each child the unhappy Leah hoped to secure her husband's affection. But each time her disappointment grew. She felt the old curse asserting itself: "Your desire will be for your husband and he will rule over you" (Genesis 3:16).

Perhaps Jacob still resented Leah for tricking him on their wedding night, disguising herself as his beloved Rachel. Surely Leah's love had been passionate enough to deceive him until morning. She felt both glad and guilty for her part; though, truth to tell, she had little choice but to obey her father, Laban, in the matter. And she thanked God each day for enabling her to bear Jacob's children. Still, children often caused a mother untold sorrow.

Dinah, her only daughter, had been raped by a local prince on their return to Jacob's homeland. Leah hardly knew how to comfort her. To make matters worse, her sons Levi and Simeon avenged their sister by savagely murdering a town-full of people. Then Reuben disgraced himself by sleeping with his father's concubine Bilhah.

Hadn't God promised to protect them if they returned to this land of promise? How, then, could such things happen? Leah wondered. True, God had watched over them as they faced Esau and his four hundred men. But Leah's joy at the brothers' friendly reunion was eclipsed by her sorrow at once again being proved the lesser-loved wife. Jacob had made it plain enough by placing Rachel and her children last in their long caravan, giving them the best chance of escape should Esau prove violent.

But Jacob's love could not prevent Rachel from dying in childbirth. Leah, not Rachel, was destined to be his first and last wife. Alongside her husband, the father of Israel, she would be revered as a mother of Israel. In fact, the promise of a Savior was carried not through Rachel's Joseph but through Leah's Judah, whose descendants would include David, Israel's great king, and Jesus, the long-awaited Messiah. In the end, Jacob was laid to rest in the Cave of Machpelah, next to his first wife, Leah, rather than his favorite wife, Rachel, who was buried somewhere near Ephrath.

The two sisters, Rachel and Leah, remind us that life is fraught with sorrow and peril, much of it caused by sin and selfishness. Both women suffered—each in her own way—the curse of Eve after she was expelled from her garden paradise. While Rachel experienced great pain in giving birth to children, Leah experienced the anguish of loving a man who seemed indifferent to her. Yet both women became mothers in Israel, leaving their homeland to play essential roles in the story of God's great plan for his people.

Her Life and Times

Marriage Customs

The customs of marriage were far different in ancient biblical times from our own modern customs. Seldom did a man or woman marry for love. Jacob is a notable exception when he expresses his love for Rachel and his desire to marry her. Jacob married both Rachel and her sister, Leah, a practice that was later forbidden by law (Leviticus 18:18).

Usually the bride and groom were very young when they married. The bride was often only around twelve and the groom around thirteen. Their marriage was arranged by parents, and their consent was neither requested nor required. Even so, such marriages could prove to be love matches, like that between Isaac and Rebekah (Genesis 24:67). By New Testament times, the marriage ceremony itself was usually very short, but the festivities connected with it could go on for many days. The groom dressed in colorful clothing and set out just before sunset, with his friends and attendants and musicians, for the home of the bride's parents. There the bride would be waiting, washed and perfumed and bedecked in an elaborate dress and jewels. The bride and groom then led the marriage procession through the village streets, accompanied by music and torchbearers, to the groom's parents' home. The feasting and celebration began that night and often continued for seven days.

God's design for marriage to be between one husband and one wife was often not practiced in early biblical times. Leah shared her husband Jacob with not only her sister, Rachel, but their maids, Zilpah and Bilhah. Although polygamy was less common after the Exodus from Egypt, Gideon had a number of wives (Judges 8:30), and, of course, Solomon had many (1 Kings 11:3). But, as the New Testament indicates, a union between one husband and one wife continues to be God's design and desire (1 Timothy 3:2, 12; Titus 1:6).

Her Legacy in Scripture

Read Genesis 29:30

1. Pick one word you think best describes how Leah felt about this marriage to Jacob.

2. Many women today have husbands who love something more than their wives: their jobs, their position, their money, sports. Many things other than another woman can put a wife in Leah's position. If you know someone who is a "Leah," pray daily for her and be an encouragement to her when given the opportunity.

Read Genesis 29:31

3. Leah is an unparalleled example of God's willingness to give "beauty" for "ashes" (see Isaiah 61:1–3). How has God worked this way in your life? How has he worked this way in the lives of your friends or relatives?

Read Genesis 29:32–34

4. In each of these verses, Leah expresses her desire for Jacob's affection, an affection she knew she didn't have. In your own words, describe how Leah probably felt and acted toward Jacob. What do you think Jacob's reaction was?

5. Have you ever felt unloved by your husband, your parents, or someone else? How did you feel and act?

What is your only possible source of comfort when you desperately want a love you don't have?

Read Genesis 49:29–31

6. Jacob was buried next to the wife he loved less rather than next to the wife he loved more. What does this say not only about Leah's position as a wife, but also as a mother of the Israelites?

7. Although Leah was, of course, unaware of the position she was awarded in death, what do these verses continue to reveal about God's involvement in her life?

8. Leah had a full life with many sons and wealth. However, she is best known for what she didn't have: the love of her husband. God noticed what she did have but also what she lacked. What one thing do you want to learn from Leah and from her God?

Her Promise

"When the LORD saw that Leah was not loved, he opened her womb" (Genesis 29:31). The Lord *noticed* Leah's misery. The God of Abraham, Isaac, and Jacob (Leah's husband) looked down and saw a woman who was lonely and sad because her husband loved his other wife better than he loved her. So, to ease her sorrow, to provide her comfort, God gave her children—beautiful, upright, strong children, one of whom would found the lineage of the priests of Israel and another who was an ancestor of Jesus himself.

This same God of Abraham, Isaac, Jacob, and Leah is our God. He sees our miseries, no matter how small or how large. He knows our circumstances, our feelings, our hurts. And, just as in Leah's life, he's willing to step in and create something beautiful in and through us.

Promises in Scripture

> *He [God] has sent me to bind up the brokenhearted,*
> *to proclaim freedom for the captives*
> *and release from darkness for the prisoners . . .*
> *and provide for those who grieve in Zion—*
> *to bestow on them a crown of beauty*
> *instead of ashes,*
> *the oil of gladness*
> *instead of mourning,*

and a garment of praise
*   instead of a spirit of despair.*

—Isaiah 61:1, 3

I will turn their mourning into gladness;
*   I will give them comfort and joy instead of sorrow.*
—Jeremiah 31:13

Her Legacy of Prayer

When the LORD saw that Leah was not loved, he opened her womb, but Rachel was barren. Leah became pregnant and gave birth to a son. She named him Reuben, for she said, "It is because the LORD has seen my misery. Surely my husband will love me now."

—Genesis 29:31 – 32

Reflect On: Genesis 29:16 – 31.

Praise God: That though human beings often judge by outward appearances, God always sees the heart and judges accordingly.

Offer Thanks: That God is moved by our sorrow.

Confess: Your tendency to compare yourself with other women, judging them and yourself merely by appearances.

Ask God: To enable you to base your identity on your relationship with him rather than on what you see in the mirror.

Lift Your Heart

Take five minutes a day this week to pay yourself a compliment by thanking God for making you the woman you are. Call to mind everything you like about yourself—your quirky sense of humor, your love of great literature, your compassion for other people, your curly hair, even the shape of your toes. Resist the temptation to think about what you don't like. (Imagine for a moment how God must feel when he hears us complaining about how he has made us!) Instead, decide now to honor him by your gratitude. At the end of the week, treat yourself to lunch with a friend or a leisurely latte at your favorite café in celebration of all the natural gifts with which God has blessed you.

Lord, I don't want to be critical of how you've put me together, relying on what others think of me for my sense of well-being. Make me a woman who is confident that I am lovable, not because of my outward beauty but because you have loved me from the moment you called me into being.

The Mothers of Moses

Jochebed: Her Name Means *The Lord Is Glory*

Her Character: Her fierce love for her son, coupled with her faith, enabled her to act heroically in the midst of great oppression.

Her Sorrow: To live in bondage as a slave.

Her Joy: That God not only preserved the son she surrendered to him but that he restored her child to her.

Key Scriptures: Exodus 2:1 – 10; Hebrews 11:23

Pharaoh's Daughter

Her Character: The Jewish people honor men and women whom they designate as "righteous Gentiles." These are people who, though nonbelievers, have assisted God's people in some significant way. Surely, Pharaoh's daughter should top the list of righteous Gentiles, courageously and compassionately delivering a child from death, a child who would one day act as Israel's great deliverer.

Her Sorrow: That her adopted son, whom she had taken care of for forty years, had to flee his home in Egypt in order to escape Pharaoh's wrath.

Key Scripture: Exodus 2:1 – 10

Their Story

Three hundred years after the death of the patriarch Joseph, a baby boy was born in Egypt, his lusty cries muffled by a woman's sobs. Jochebed's heart was a tangle of joy and fear. This son, his fingers forming a tiny fist against her breast, was so striking a child she hardly believed he was hers. Tenderly she raised the small hand to her mouth, pressing its warmth to her lips. Her gesture calmed them both. She could feel the stiffness in her back dissolving, her muscles relaxing as she watched the night shadows evaporate in the morning's light.

Slave though she was, she was yet a Levite, a woman who belonged to the God of Abraham and Sarah, of Isaac and Rebekah, of Jacob, Rachel, and Leah. She knew the stories. She believed the promises. God was faithful. Hadn't her people already grown as numerous as the sand of the sea, just as he had said they would?

In fact, the Israelites were so numerous that the pharaohs feared they might one day welcome an invading army and betray the nation from within. Over time, the Egyptians had tightened their grip, finally enslaving the Israelites, until Pharaoh's paranoia produced an even greater evil—a command to murder each Hebrew male child emerging from the womb. But the Hebrew midwives feared God more than the king and refused to follow his orders, excusing themselves by claiming that Hebrew women were stronger than Egyptian women, giving birth before the midwives even arrived.

So Pharaoh commanded his soldiers to search out and smother every newborn male in the waters of the Nile. Jochebed could hear the screams of the mothers echoing regularly across the Hebrew camp as their children were torn from them. Her arms tightened around her own child as he slept quietly against her breast. This one, she vowed, would never be fodder for the Egyptian river god. She and her husband, Amram, would pray. They would plan. And they would trust God to help them.

For three months, as long as she dared, she hid the infant, managing to keep Miriam and three-year-old Aaron quiet about their new baby brother. Finally, she acted on an idea that had been growing in her mind. Pharaoh had commanded her to consign her son to the Nile River. All right then. Her own hands would put him into the water.

Remembering how God had spared the child Isaac on the mountain of sacrifice, she bent down and laid her son in a basket of papyrus, waterproofed with tar and pitch. Then, with a whispered prayer and a last caress, she wiped her eyes, begging God to preserve her baby from the crocodiles that swarmed the river.

She could not bear to watch as the child drifted away from her. Instead, young Miriam kept vigil, following at a distance to see what would become of him.

Soon Pharaoh's daughter arrived at the riverbank with some of her attendants. Spotting the basket among the reeds, she sent her slave girl to fetch it. As soon as she beheld the brown-eyed baby, she loved him. The river had brought her a child whom she would cherish as her own. She could not save all the innocent children, but she could spare one mother's son.

Was she surprised when a young slave girl, Miriam, approached, asking whether she could go after a Hebrew woman to nurse the baby for her? Did she suspect the truth when Jochebed gathered the boy in her arms, this time as his nursemaid?

Whatever was in her mind, she named the child Moses, saying, "I drew him out of the water." For the next forty years, she educated him, a prince in the courts of Pharaoh himself.

God kept Moses safe in the very midst of extraordinary evil and danger—first in crocodile-infested waters and then right under Pharaoh's nose. And he used the Egyptians to protect and educate him in ways that must have made Moses even more effective in his eventual role as his people's deliverer.

Year after year, Jochebed would surely have reflected on the marvelous faithfulness of God. Her ingenuity, courage, and faith should inspire even the most weak-kneed among us.

Two women—a slave and a princess—preserved the life of Israel's future deliverer and so preserved the entire Jewish race.

Their Life and Times

Baskets

Such an ordinary object, used to such extraordinary purpose. Imagine with what love and care Jochebed coated the papyrus basket with tar and pitch before placing her precious son within it. Few baskets throughout the centuries likely received as loving and careful a touch.

Baskets were just one of the many types of vessels used to store and carry various items in the ancient world. In the home, women used baskets to store household items as well as fruit and bread. Brick makers carried their clay in baskets. Travelers used them to carry the supplies they needed for their journey. Priests in Israel used baskets to store the bread and wafers that were a part of worship in the tabernacle (Exodus 29:3, 23, 32).

Typically made from some sort of plant material — leaves, twigs, or stalks — baskets came in a variety of shapes and sizes. The smallest could be carried in one hand. Baskets just a bit larger were carried on the back or on the head and were often used to hold provisions on a trip. The disciples used twelve of these large baskets to gather up the leftovers at the feeding of the five thousand (Matthew 14:20). An even larger basket was used to let Paul escape out of a window in the wall at Damascus (Acts 9:25), so it must have been quite large and sturdy.

God's use of the ordinary to bring about the extraordinary is as much in evidence here in the early events of Exodus as anywhere in Scripture. His tendency to bring about his will through ordinary items, ordinary people, and ordinary events is no less at work today than it was in Jochebed's. If you look for the signs of his presence, you are sure to discover them.

Their Legacy in Scripture

Read Exodus 2:1 – 2

1. In your own words describe the events of these two verses. Look behind the scenes. How do you think the family kept the baby quiet? If a close neighbor heard the newborn's cries, what do you think he or she would have done? What if that neighbor had herself just lost a newborn to Pharaoh's decrees? Why at three months could Jochebed "hide him no longer"?

2. How do you think you would have reacted in these circumstances? Like Jochebed? Like the other mothers?

Read Exodus 2:3 – 4

3. The events here go straight to a mother's heart. How do you think Jochebed felt as she walked away from the river?

Read Exodus 2:5 – 6

4. Pharaoh's daughter, a member of the royal family, part of the race that was oppressing the Israelites, now enters the picture. What is most obvious about her from these verses?

5. Why do you suppose she was allowed to disobey her father's harsh edict?

Read Exodus 2:7–10

6. Compare verses 9 and 10. What conflicting emotions do you think Jochebed must have felt?

Reread Exodus 2:10

7. What is the significance of the words "he [Moses] became her son"?

8. What purpose of God was at work here?

Read Hebrews 11:23

9. This verse says that Moses' mother and father acted "by faith." Their one goal was to protect and save their child. Fear for our children's safety—for their spiritual and physical lives—seems to be an inescapable part of parenting. What part does faith play in child rearing? What is your greatest fear for your child? How can you "by faith" respond to your fears?

Their Promise

Moses' mother, Jochebed, had one thing in mind when hiding her son and leaving him in a basket in the river. Her goal was to preserve his life for one more day, one more hour, one more moment. She could not have known how God planned to work in her life or in the life of her son. Nor did she realize he was putting into place a divine plan to rescue his people from the very oppression she was resisting.

God's ways are beautiful in the extreme. He uses the devoted, intense love of a mother for her child to bring freedom to an entire race. Like Jochebed, our goal should be to hang on, trusting that God has his own purpose at work and that we and our children are part of it.

Promises in Scripture

> *The plans of the LORD stand firm forever,*
> *the purposes of his heart through all generations....*
> *The eyes of the LORD are on those who fear him,*
> *on those whose hope is in his unfailing love.*
> —Psalm 33:11, 18

> *"For I know the plans I have for you," declares the LORD,*
> *"plans to prosper you and not to harm you, plans to give*
> *you hope and a future. Then you will call upon me and*
> *come and pray to me, and I will listen to you. You will*
> *seek me and find me when you seek me with all your*
> *heart. I will be found by you," declares the LORD.*
> —Jeremiah 29:11–14

Their Legacy of Prayer

When she could hide him no longer, she got a papyrus basket for him and coated it with tar and pitch. Then she placed the child in it and put it among the reeds along the bank of the Nile.

—Exodus 2:3

Reflect On: Exodus 2:1 – 10.

Praise God: That even the worst enemies we encounter are weak compared to him.

Offer Thanks: For God's power to save.

Confess: Any failure to trust God for the lives of our children.

Ask God: To help you be an encouragement to another mother who is concerned about her children's well-being.

Lift Your Heart

Find another mother, perhaps a teenage mom or a friend who is having difficulty with her own children right now. Put together a gift basket for her, filled with small gifts like a scented candle, dried fruit, a coffee cup, and some small cards inscribed with encouraging Scripture verses. Tell her you will be praying for each of her children by name every day for the next couple of months. Don't expect her to confide in you, but if she does, cherish what she tells you by keeping it confidential and letting it shape your prayers.

Father, thank you for the gift and calling of motherhood. Help me to remember that my love for my children is merely a reflection of your own love for them. With that in mind, give me grace to surrender my anxiety. Replace it with a sense of trust and calm as I learn to depend on you for everything. Amen.

Hannah

Her Name Means *Graciousness* or *Favor*

Her Character:	Provoked by another woman's malice, she refused to respond in kind. Instead, she poured out her hurt and sorrow to God, allowing him to vindicate her.
Her Sorrow:	To be taunted and misunderstood.
Her Joy:	To proclaim God's power and goodness, his habit of raising the lowly and humbling the proud.
Key Scriptures:	1 Samuel 1:1 – 2:11; 2:19 – 21

Her Story

It was only fifteen miles, but every year the journey from Ramah, to worship at the tabernacle in Shiloh, seemed longer. At home, Hannah found ways to avoid her husband's second wife, but once in Shiloh there was no escaping her taunts. Hannah felt like a leaky tent in a driving rain, unable to defend herself against the harsh weather of the other woman's heart.

Even Elkanah's arm around her provided no shelter. "Hannah, why are you weeping? Why don't you eat? Why are you downhearted? Don't I mean more to you than ten sons? Yes, she has given me children, but it's you I love. Ignore her taunts."

How could Hannah make him understand that even the best of men could not erase a woman's longing for children? His attempt at comforting her only sharpened the pain, heightening her sense of isolation.

Hannah stood for a long time at the tabernacle, weeping and praying. Her lips moved without making a sound as her heart poured out its grief to God: "O LORD Almighty, if you will only look upon your servant's misery and remember me, and not forget your servant but give her a son, then I will give him to the LORD for all the days of his life, and no razor will ever be used on his head."

The priest Eli was used to people coming to Shiloh to celebrate the feasts, eating and drinking more than they should. Watching Hannah from his chair by the doorpost of the temple, he wondered why her shoulders were shaking, her lips moving without making a sound. She must be drunk, he concluded. So he interrupted her silent prayer with a rebuke: "How long will you keep on getting drunk? Get rid of your wine."

"Not so, my lord," Hannah defended herself. "I am a woman who is deeply troubled. I have not been drinking wine or beer; I was pouring out my soul to the LORD. Do not take your servant for a wicked woman; I have been praying here out of my great anguish and grief."

Satisfied by her explanation, Eli blessed her, saying, "May the God of Israel grant your request."

Early the next morning, Hannah and Elkanah returned to their home in Ramah, where Hannah at last conceived. Soon she held against her shoulder the tiny child she had yearned for, the son she had dedicated to God. After Samuel was weaned, she took him to Eli at Shiloh. Like Jochebed placing the child Moses into the waters of the Nile as though into God's own hands, she surrendered her child to the priest's care. Eventually Hannah's boy would become prophet and Israel's last judge. His hands would anoint both Saul and David as Israel's first kings.

Like Sarah and Rachel, Hannah grieved over the children she could not have. But unlike them, she took her anguish directly to God. Misunderstood by both her husband and her priest, she could easily have turned her sorrow on herself or others, becoming bitter, hopeless, or vindictive. But instead of merely pitying herself or responding in kind, she poured out her soul to God. And God graciously answered her prayer.

Each year Hannah went up to Shiloh and presented Samuel with a little robe she had sewn. And each year, the priest Eli blessed her husband, Elkanah, saying, "May the LORD give you children by this woman to take the place of the one she prayed for and gave to the LORD." And so Hannah became the mother of three more sons and two daughters.

Her great prayer, echoed nearly a thousand years later by Mary, the mother of Jesus (Luke 1:46–55), expresses Hannah's praise: "My heart rejoices in the LORD; in the LORD my horn is lifted high. My mouth boasts over my enemies, for I delight in your deliverance.... The Lord sends poverty and wealth; he humbles and he exalts. He raises the poor from the dust and lifts the needy from the ash heap."

Her Life and Times

Infertility

Praying through her tears, so overwrought that Eli thought she was drunk, Hannah expresses for women throughout the ages the agonizing experience of infertility. The deep, unsatisfied longing for children, the pain of watching others bear one child after another, the anguish of watching a mother kiss her baby's face — Hannah experienced them all.

The Israelites saw children as a particular blessing from the Lord, recognizing his power to open or close a woman's womb. Women who couldn't bear children were considered subfemale, unable to fulfill their divine purpose on earth. When a woman was unable to fulfill this "duty," her emotional pain was tremendous. And more than likely, barren women also felt they were denied the possibility of being the one chosen to bear the Messiah.

Infertility brought with it not only a debilitating personal sorrow but also the reproach of a woman's husband, the disapproval of a woman's family, and the rejection of society. Husbands looked to their wives to produce many sons to help in supporting the family. A woman's extended family, both her own and her husband's, looked to her to continue the family line and saw her as one who had not fulfilled her responsibility when she didn't produce children. And the social circles of young women of childbearing years by their very nature included many other young women, women who were often producing one child after another. Their fertility mocked the infertility of the barren woman every time she went to the market or to the well or to a community social event.

Scripture tells the stories of a number of women who were barren. Sarah laughed when told she would finally have a son. Rachel clutched Jacob and begged him to give her sons, as if he could open her womb. Hannah's pain made her seek help from the only One truly capable of providing it.

If Hannah had never had a child, she would still have gone down in Scripture's narrative as a woman of faith. Hannah is not a woman of faith because she bore a child; she is a woman of faith because she sought God when she was in her deepest distress, because she realized that only he could answer her questions and that only he could provide the consolation and purpose in life she so desperately sought.

Her Legacy in Scripture

Read 1 Samuel 1:1–8

1. What sort of response does Hannah's childlessness cause in each of the people involved: in Hannah herself? in Peninnah? in Elkanah?
2. How have you reacted to disappointments or failures in your life?
3. What impact did the reactions of those around you have on you?

Read 1 Samuel 1:9–14

4. Hannah stood in this very public place and poured out her pain to the Lord. Notice Eli's reaction. Do you think she was unaware of the reaction others may have had, or do you think she just didn't care?

Read 1 Samuel 1:15–18

5. What caused the change in Hannah recorded in verse 18? Is there anything here that would make her sure she would now bear a son? If not, why then was she comforted?
6. When has God answered your prayers after a time of disappointment or difficulty? When have your prayers gone unanswered? How did God provide in those troublesome times?

Read 1 Samuel 1:19–20

7. How did God answer Hannah's prayer? What is the significance of the name Samuel?

Read 1 Samuel 1:21–28

8. These verses record Hannah's fulfillment to her vow, recorded in verse 11. What would have made Hannah's vow difficult? What would have made it necessary?

Read 1 Samuel 2:18–21

9. Describe Hannah's actions during the years when Samuel was growing up in the temple. What do you think those years were like for her?

10. How did God reward Hannah for her faithfulness?

11. Hannah dedicated her son Samuel to the Lord by giving him up to the Lord and to the work in the temple. Are your children dedicated to the Lord? If so, what are you doing to help them grow up in him?

Her Promise

When God met Hannah at the temple in Shiloh, he not only answered her prayer for a child, he answered her prayer for comfort in her misery. He gave her consolation in her disappointment and strength to face her situation. Scripture does not say that she went away sure she would bear a child, but it does make it clear that she went away comforted: "Her face was no longer downcast" (1 Samuel 1:18). What even the love and care of her husband Elkanah could not provide, God could provide.

God is willing to meet us just as he met Hannah. Whatever our distress, whatever hard situations we face, he is willing — more than that, he is eager — to meet our needs and give us his grace and comfort. No other person — not our husband, not our closest friends, not our parents, not our children — can render the relief, support, and encouragement that our God has waiting for us.

Promises in Scripture

My comfort in my suffering is this:
Your promise preserves my life.

—Psalm 119:50

We rejoice in the hope of the glory of God. Not only so, but we also rejoice in our sufferings, because we know that suffering produces perseverance; perseverance, character; and character, hope. And hope does not disappoint us, because God has poured out his love into our hearts by the Holy Spirit, whom he has given us.

—Romans 5:2–5

And we know that in all things God works for the good of those who love him, who have been called according to his purpose.

—Romans 8:28

FRIDAY

Her Legacy of Prayer

*In bitterness of soul Hannah wept much and prayed to the LORD.
And she made a vow, saying, "O LORD Almighty, if you will only
look upon your servant's misery and remember me, and not forget
your servant but give her a son, then I will give him to the LORD
for all the days of his life."*

—1 Samuel 1:10–11

Reflect On: 1 Samuel 2:1–10.

Praise God: That he knows our hearts.

Offer Thanks: For already answering so many of your prayers.

Confess: Your tendency to pour out your heart to everyone but God, making him a last, rather than first, resort.

Ask God: To give you the grace to trust his strength.

Lift Your Heart

One way to build your confidence in God is to form a habit of remembrance. It's so easy to forget everything he's already done by being preoccupied with what you want him to do right here, right now. But by forgetting his blessings, you form a habit of ingratitude. By frequently thanking God for what he's done, you build a habit of gratitude, which will also deepen your trust in God's compassion, mercy, faithfulness, and power.

Find a blank notebook or a lovely scrapbook that can become your Remembrance Book. In it, write down ways in which God has answered your prayers. Keep letters, photos of loved ones, or newspaper clippings—anything that reminds you of answered prayers. Let your Remembrance Book be a tangible way of keeping God's faithfulness in the forefront of your heart.

Father, thank you for all the prayers you've answered during my lifetime. You've answered small prayers and big prayers, evening prayers and morning prayers, soft prayers and loud prayers, anxious prayers and peaceful prayers. May my own prayers be shaped according to your faithfulness, becoming less selfish and frantic and more calm and trusting with each day that passes. In Jesus' name, Amen.

Elizabeth

Her Name Means *God Is My Oath*

Her Character: A descendant of Aaron, Elizabeth was a woman the Bible calls "upright in the sight of God." Like few others, male or female, she was praised for observing all the Lord's commandments and regulations without blame. She was the first to acknowledge Jesus as Lord.

Her Sorrow: To be barren for most of her life.

Her Joy: To give birth to John, later known as John the Baptist, the Messiah's forerunner. His name, divinely assigned, means, "The Lord is gracious."

Key Scripture: Luke 1:5–80

Her Story

Her eyes were a golden brown. Like currants set in pastry, they winked out at the world from cheeks that had baked too long in the sun. Snowy strands of hair straggled from beneath a woolen shawl, tickling her wrinkled face. Small hands rested tenderly on her rounded belly, softly probing for any hint of movement. But all was still. From her vantage point on the roof of the house, she noticed a figure walking up the pathway and wondered who her visitor might be.

She and Zechariah had been content enough in their quiet house these last few months, secluded in their joy. Each morning she had opened her eyes as though waking to a fantastic dream. Sometimes she shook with laughter as she thought about how God had rearranged her life, planting a child in her shriveled up, old-woman's womb.

Six months ago, Zechariah had been chosen by lot to burn incense before the Most Holy Place, a once-in-a-lifetime privilege. But during his week of priestly service in the temple, he had been frightened half to death by a figure that appeared suddenly next to the altar of incense. "Your wife Elizabeth will bear you a son," the angel told him, "and you are to give him the name John. He will be a joy and delight to you, and many will rejoice because of his birth, for he will be great in the sight of the Lord." It was Sarah and Abraham all over, Rebekah and Isaac, Rachel and Jacob. God was once again kindling a fire with two dry sticks.

For the life of her, Elizabeth couldn't understand her husband's response to the angel that had so terrified him. Once you'd laid eyes on a heavenly being, how could you fail to believe that anything was possible? But Zechariah had blurted out his skepticism and suffered the consequences. His voice had been snatched away and would not be given back until the angel's words came to pass. These days he communicated by scribbling on a wax tablet.

Elizabeth looked down again at the figure advancing up the path, a green sprig of a girl. The older woman stepped carefully down the stairs and into the house to welcome her guest. But with the young woman's words of greeting came something that felt like a gale force wind, shaking the beams and rafters of the house. Steadying herself, the older woman felt suddenly invigorated. Her unborn baby leapt inside her as she shouted out a welcoming response:

"Blessed are you among women, and blessed is the child you will bear! But why am I so favored, that the mother of my Lord should come to me? As soon as the sound of your greeting reached my ears, the baby in my womb leaped for joy. Blessed is she who has believed that what the Lord has said to her will be accomplished!"

Mary had made the journey all the way from Nazareth to visit her relative, Elizabeth. The same angel who had spoken to Zechariah in the temple had whispered the secret of the older woman's pregnancy to the virgin, who was also with child. The magnificent song of praise that burst from Mary's lips during their meeting may have taken shape during the course of her sixty-mile journey south, to the hill country of Judea where Elizabeth lived:

My soul glorifies the Lord
    and my spirit rejoices in God my Savior,
for he has been mindful
    of the humble state of his servant.
From now on all generations will call me blessed,
    for the Mighty One has done great things for me—
    holy is his name.
His mercy extends to those who fear him,
    from generation to generation.
He has performed mighty deeds with his arm;
    he has scattered those who are proud in their inmost
    thoughts.
He has brought down rulers from their thrones
    but has lifted up the humble.
He has filled the hungry with good things
    but has sent the rich away empty.
He has helped his servant Israel,
    remembering to be merciful
to Abraham and his descendants forever,
    even as he said to our fathers.

The two women held each other, their bonds of kinship now so much stronger than what mere flesh and blood could forge. For Israel's God—the God of Sarah, Rebekah, Rachel, Leah, Miriam, Deborah, Naomi, Ruth, Abigail, and Hannah—was on the move again, bringing the long-ago promise to fulfillment. And blessed was she who did not doubt that what the Lord had said to her would be accomplished.

Her Life and Times

Incense

Elizabeth's husband, Zechariah, had been given a special, very serious privilege. When it was his priestly division's turn to serve in the temple, he was chosen by lot — which was God's way of making the choice — to burn incense in the temple. Each morning and evening he took fire from the altar of burnt offering and placed it on the golden altar of incense that stood before the curtain separating the Holy Place from the Most Holy Place. He then poured the dusty incense from a golden urn onto the fire. While Zechariah performed this duty, all the worshipers who were at the temple that day stood outside and prayed. The smoke and aroma of the incense symbolized their prayers rising up to God. The fragrance also served to fumigate air tainted with the odor of the blood of animals killed for the sacrifices.

The earliest historical records about worship include information on the burning of incense. All the nations surrounding Palestine appreciated the sweet smell of incense permeating not only their places of worship but also their homes. The incense Zechariah burned in the temple was made according to a special "recipe" (Exodus 30:34–38) of spices and salt that had been ground to a powder. This holy incense could be used only in the temple in worship, never for ordinary, everyday purposes.

The prophet Jeremiah often condemned the Israelites for burning incense to false gods. But he could be even more scathing in his denunciation when they burned incense when their hearts weren't in their worship (Jeremiah 6:20). God made it clear that the mere burning of incense didn't please him; it was only a symbol. He was looking for hearts that were turned toward him with faithfulness and trust.

Isn't that application obvious for us today as well? In all our forms of worship—our hymns and praise songs, our liturgies and dramas and readings—what is important to God is our hearts. Are they turned toward him in faithfulness and trust?

Her Legacy in Scripture

Read Luke 1:5–7

1. What important things do these verses tell you about Elizabeth and Zechariah? Do you think the words of verse 6 mean they were perfect? If not, what *do* these words mean?

Read Luke 1:8–22

2. Why do you think Zechariah didn't believe the angel? Was he so afraid? Was the announcement so unbelievable? Why do you think he was punished for not believing?

3. Imagine an angel coming to you with some unexpected and unbelievable announcement. What would your reaction be?

Read Luke 1:23–25

4. Why would Elizabeth say she was disgraced among her people?

5. Describe how the infertile woman feels today. Is disgrace a part of her feelings? If you know someone who is struggling with infertility, how can you be a friend and support to her?

Read Luke 1:39–41

6. Do you think the reaction of Elizabeth's baby to Mary's arrival was just coincidence? What do you think prompted the baby to "leap" just then?

Read Luke 1:42–44

7. Elizabeth didn't just smile and offer a quiet prayer when Mary arrived. She "exclaimed" and praised God "in a loud voice." What would have to happen for you to exclaim your praise to God in a loud voice?

Read Luke 1:45

8. What is the focus of Elizabeth's praise: what God has done in *her* life or what God has done in *Mary's* life? What does this reveal about Elizabeth?

THURSDAY

Her Promise

God always keeps his promises! For hundreds of years, God had been telling the people of Israel that he would send a Messiah. One who would do away with all the sacrifices and priesthood. One who would provide a direct bridge to God himself. One whose sacrifice would provide redemption for all time. The events in this first chapter of Luke are just the beginning of the fulfillment of God's greatest promise to his people. With Mary we can say: "My soul glorifies the Lord and my spirit rejoices in God my Savior!"

Promises in Scripture

But for you who revere my name, the sun of righteousness will rise with healing in its wings. And you will go out and leap like calves released from the stall.

—Malachi 4:2

John saw Jesus coming toward him and said, "Look, the Lamb of God, who takes away the sin of the world!"

—John 1:29

Here is a trustworthy saying that deserves full acceptance: Christ Jesus came into the world to save sinners.

—1 Timothy 1:15

Her Legacy of Prayer

Blessed is she who has believed that what the Lord has said to her will be accomplished!

—Luke 1:45

Reflect On: Luke 1:5–80.

Praise God: That he is the Creator who shapes every child in the womb.

Offer Thanks: For the gift of children.

Confess: Any tendency to cheapen the value of human life, including unborn life.

Ask God: To restore our appreciation for the miracle of human life.

Lift Your Heart

A person's a person, no matter how small!
—From *Horton Hears a Who* by Dr. Seuss

Mary's visit to Elizabeth probably occurred when Elizabeth was in her sixth month of pregnancy. The younger woman may have stayed long enough to help the older one with her delivery. In any case, Mary would have been in the first trimester of her pregnancy and Elizabeth in her third.

Here's what would have been happening to the children growing in their wombs:

Jesus:

18 days — his nervous system appeared.

30 days — most of his major organ systems had begun to form.

4 weeks — his heart began beating.

7 weeks — his facial features would have been visible.

8th week — all his major body structures and organs were present.

10th week — tiny teeth were forming in his gums.

12th week — his brain was fully formed and he could feel pain. He may have even sucked his thumb.

John:

6th month — he could grasp his hands, kick, do somersaults, and hear voices and sounds outside the womb.

Take a few moments to praise your Creator with beautiful words from Psalm 139:13–16:

For you created my inmost being;
*   you knit me together in my mother's womb.*
I praise you because I am fearfully and wonderfully made;
*   your works are wonderful,*
*   I know that full well.*
My frame was not hidden from you
*   when I was made in the secret place.*
When I was woven together in the depths of the earth,
*   your eyes saw my unformed body.*

All the days ordained for me were written in your book
before one of them came to be.

Dear God, you are the Lord and Giver of life. Help me to respect,
protect, and nurture it no matter what color, no matter what
age, no matter what gender of human being I encounter. I ask
this in the name of Jesus, the bread and water of life, Amen.

Mary, the Mother of Jesus
Her Name May Mean *Bitterness*

Her Character: She was a virgin from a poor family in an obscure village in Galilee. Her response to Gabriel reveals a young woman of unusual faith and humility. Her unqualified yes to God's plan for her life entailed great personal risk and suffering. She must have endured seasons of confusion, fear, and darkness as the events of her life unfolded. She is honored, not only as the mother of Jesus, but as his first disciple.

Her Sorrow: To see the son she loved shamed and tortured, left to die like the worst kind of criminal.

Her Joy: To see her child raised from the dead; to have received the Holy Spirit along with Christ's other disciples.

Key Scriptures: Matthew 1:18–25; 2; Luke 1:26–80; 2; John 19:25–27

MONDAY

Her Story

She sat down on the bench and closed her eyes, an old woman silhouetted against the blue Jerusalem sky. Even the wood beneath her conjured images. Though she could no longer recall the exact curl of his smile or the shape of his sleeping face resting next to hers, she could still see the rough brown hands, expertly molding the wood to his purposes. Joseph had been a good carpenter and an even better husband.

These days the memories came unbidden, like a gusty wind carrying her away to other times and places. Some said drowning people see their lives unfold in incredible detail just before they die. Age had a similar effect, she thought, except that you could relive your memories with a great deal more leisure....

A cool breeze teased at her skirts as she balanced the jug on her head, making her way toward the well. A stranger, she noticed, was approaching from the opposite direction. Even in the dusky light, his clothes shone, as though bleached bright by the strongest of fuller's soap.

"Greetings," he shouted, "you who are highly favored! The Lord is with you."

No Nazarene, she was sure, would ever dare greet a maiden like that. But with each step his words grew bolder, not softer, rushing toward her as water plunges over a cliff:

> "Do not be afraid, Mary. . . .
>> You have found favor with God. . . .
>> You will give birth to a son. . . .
>>> He will be called the Son of the Most High. . . .
>>> The Holy Spirit will come upon you. . . .
>>>> Elizabeth your relative is going to have a child in her old age."

Wave after wave broke over her as she listened to the angel's words—first confusion and fear, then awe and gratitude, and finally a rush of joy and peace. Her whole being drenched in light. Then she heard more words, this time cascading from her lips, not his:

> "I am the Lord's servant.
> May it be to me as you have said."

Though the angel departed, Mary's peace remained. The Most High had visited the lowliest of his servants and spoken the promise every Jewish woman longed to hear: "You will be with child and give birth to a son, and you are to give him the name Jesus. The Lord God will give him the throne of his father David, and he will reign over the house of Jacob forever; his kingdom will never end."

The moon hung like a smile in the night sky as she lifted the brimming buckets and began walking across the fields. As the water swayed and splashed to the rhythm of her movements, she realized that she too felt full and satisfied—as though she had just finished a favorite meal. Questions, she knew, would come with the morning. For now, it was enough to look up at the stars and know that God was at work shaping her future.

"Mama, Mama," he yelled, running toward her, chubby arms flung out beseechingly.

"Jesus, what is it now, child?" she smiled, scooping the chunky boy into her arms before he could topple over in the usual tangle of arms and legs. But he was all kisses, squealing and nuzzling his curly head against her breast, as though to bury himself in her soft, warm flesh. She sighed contentedly. How many mothers had she known? But none had adequately described the sheer wonder of a child—the laughter, the constant surprise, the tenderness. Not to mention the fear and worry that were also part of the bargain.

But this was no time to entertain such thoughts. The men from the East had recently left. How strange these Magi seemed, with their tales of a star that had led them all the way to Bethlehem in search of a new king. They had bowed before her dark-eyed child, laying out their treasures of gold, incense, and myrrh—as though paying homage to royalty. One morning, however, they had packed in haste, saying only that a dream had warned them to return home without reporting news of their successful search to the king. Even the mention of Herod's name had filled her with dread. Bethlehem lay just six miles south of Jerusalem—dangerously close to a man who had murdered his own children out of jealousy for his throne. How would such a ruler respond to rumors of a child-king in Bethlehem?

Two nights ago Joseph had shaken her awake, shushing her with details of the dream he had just had: "Mary, an angel appeared to me. We must leave before sunrise. Herod plans to search for our child and kill him!"

Now they were on their way to Egypt, reversing the steps of Moses, Aaron, and Miriam, who had led her ancestors to freedom so long ago. Mary wondered, as they rested, if they would ever see their homeland again.

***

"Woman," he breathed the word softly, painfully, through lips encrusted with blood, his lean arms flung out on either side of him, as though imploringly. The palms of his hands were pinned with spikes. He looked at her first and then at the young man standing beside her. "Here is your son." The words came haltingly.

Then to the man, he sighed: "Here is your mother."

She wanted to reach for him with all the might of her love, to bury his sorrow in her breasts, to tell him he was the son she needed most. Would not the God who pitied Abraham also pity her? Would he allow her to suffer what even the patriarch had been spared—the sacrifice of a child? All her life she had loved the God whose angel had spoken to her, calling her "highly favored." But how could a woman whose son was dying on a Roman cross ever consider herself "favored"?

Suddenly her own words came back to her, as though a younger version of herself was whispering them in her ear: "I am the Lord's servant. May it be to me as you have said."

The midday sky had blackened, but she could still see her son's twisted form on the cross, his eyes searching hers. Thorns circled his forehead in the shape of a crown, a crude reminder of the sign the Roman governor had fastened to the wood: "Jesus of Nazareth, King of the Jews."

She thought of the Magi and their priceless gifts. The gold and incense, royal treasures that had helped them survive their stay in Egypt. She had always wondered about the myrrh. Now she knew — it was embalming oil for the king the wise men had come to worship.

"My God, my God, why have you forsaken me?" His cry pierced her like a sword. The earth shook violently and she fell to her knees, barely able to complete the words of the psalm for the man who hung dead on the cross:

"O my God, I cry out by day, but you do not answer,
　　by night, and am not silent. . . .
But I am a worm and not a man,
　　scorned by men and despised by the people.
All who see me mock me;
　　they hurl insults, shaking their heads. . . .
Yet you brought me out of the womb;
　　you made me trust in you
　　even at my mother's breast.
From birth I was cast upon you;
　　from my mother's womb you have been my God. . . .
　　they have pierced my hands and my feet.
I can count all my bones;
　　people stare and gloat over me,
They divide my garments among them
　　and cast lots for my clothing.
But you, O LORD, be not far off;
　　O my Strength, come quickly to help me. . . .

You who fear the L ORD, praise him!
All you descendants of Jacob, honor him!...
future generations will be told about the Lord.
They will proclaim his righteousness
to a people yet unborn—
for he has done it.

—Psalm 22

By the time Mary opened her eyes, the setting sun had turned the city into a golden land. She smiled, wiping the tears from her wrinkled face. How true the angel's words had been. No woman from Eve onward had ever been blessed as she, the mother of the Messiah, had been. Yes, the past was alive inside her, but it was the future that filled her with joy. Soon, she would see her son again and this time it would be *his* hands that would wipe away the last of her tears.

Her Life and Times

Angels

Mary cowered in fear when the angel Gabriel appeared to her—not an uncommon reaction. Most often in Scripture, when an angel appeared to a human being, the reaction was one of fright. While we're not told exactly what angels look like or how they appear, one description in Matthew says the angel's "appearance was like lightning, and his clothes were white as snow" (Matthew 28:3). Certainly it's obvious from the reactions of those who saw them that angels are supernatural beings and therefore frightening.

The 291 references to angels in Scripture give us a varied picture of their duties. Angels in heaven stand before God's throne and worship him (Matthew 18:10). An angel helped Hagar and Ishmael when they were in trouble in the desert (Genesis 21:17). An angel freed the apostles from prison (Acts 5:19). An angel directed Philip to the desert road where he met and witnessed to the Ethiopian eunuch (Acts 8:26). An angel appeared to Paul to comfort him (Acts 27:23–24), to Elijah when he was worn out and discouraged in the desert (1 Kings 19:3–9), and to Daniel and his friends in places of danger (Daniel 3:28; 6:22). Sometimes God uses angels to punish his enemies (Genesis 19:1; 2 Kings 19:35).

Angels played an important role in the life of Jesus. After first appearing to Zechariah, Mary, and Joseph, angels announced Jesus' birth to the shepherds (Luke 2:9). Angels came and ministered to Jesus after he was tempted in the desert (Matthew 4:11) and when he was in the garden just before his crucifixion (Luke 22:43). A violent earthquake accompanied the angel that came to earth and rolled back the stone over Jesus' tomb (Matthew 28:2). When Jesus ascended into heaven, two angels, "men dressed in white" (Acts 1:10), told the disciples he would be coming back in the same way.

In the book of Revelation, John describes a glorious scene: "Then I looked and heard the voice of many angels, numbering thousands upon thousands, and ten thousand times ten thousand. They encircled the throne and the living creatures and the elders. In a loud voice they sang: 'Worthy is the Lamb, who was slain, to receive power and wealth and wisdom and strength and honor and glory and praise!'" (Revelation 5:11–12).

Imagine the sight: hundreds of thousands of beings—purest white, like lightning—all moving in concert around God's throne. Listen: Can you imagine their loud, supernatural voices praising Jesus? *Worthy is the Lamb!* Then "every creature in heaven and on earth and under the earth and on the sea, and all that is in them" (Revelation 5:13) will join in with them, singing the same song of praise. What a sight! What a sound! Mary will be there praising her son. Will you be there praising your Savior?

Her Legacy in Scripture

Read Luke 1:26–35

1. Put the angel's greetings into your own words. Why do you think this greeting troubled Mary?

2. If an angel were to visit you today, what sort of greeting do you think he would give you? What would the greeting reveal about your character and about your relationship with God?

Read Luke 1:36–37

3. What two things does the angel tell Mary in these verses? Why would he tell her about Elizabeth? Why would he tell her that "nothing is impossible with God"? Didn't Mary already know this?

4. If truly "nothing is impossible with God," what area of your life or circumstance do you need to turn over to him? What is keeping you from doing this?

Read Luke 1:38

5. What does Mary's response tell you about her? Do you think at this point she truly realizes what her future holds? How will the attitude apparent in these words help her in the difficult times in the future?

Read Luke 2:1–7

6. These words are so familiar and the story so well-known. The birth of God on earth becomes commonplace,

ordinary. Reread these verses, considering while you do the emotions Joseph and Mary must have experienced, what they may have said to each other, how they may have prayed. Then contemplate the actual event: not just the birth of a baby but the birth of the Christ!

Read Luke 2:41–52

7. Whom does Mary call Jesus' father? Who does Jesus say his father is? Why is this significant?

8. Verse 51 says Mary and Joseph "did not understand" what Jesus meant by what he said to them. However, verse 51 says that Mary "treasured all these things in her heart." Contrast the two verses. What do you think is meant by "treasured"?

Read John 19:25–27

9. It is hard to put into words the agony Mary must have been experiencing as she watched her son die. Seeing her distress must have added to Jesus' torment. What does this scene tell you about their relationship?

10. Watching a son or daughter die is perhaps the most painful experience known to the human race. Where is the only place to go to find comfort when such painful events enter our lives? Why?

Her Promise

When God says nothing is impossible, he means it. He is all-powerful, omnipotent, the Savior of the world. No matter what he has promised, no matter how hard or impossible that promise seems to fulfill, he can and will do it.

Promises in Scripture

For the LORD your God dried up the Jordan before you until you had crossed over.... He did this so that all the peoples of the earth might know that the hand of the LORD is powerful and so that you might always fear the LORD your God.

—Joshua 4:23–24

With man this is impossible, but with God all things are possible.

—Matthew 19:26

For the foolishness of God is wiser than man's wisdom, and the weakness of God is stronger than man's strength.

—1 Corinthians 1:25

Her Legacy of Prayer

"Greetings, you who are highly favored! The Lord is with you."
—Luke 1:28

Reflect On: Luke 1:26–38.

Praise God: That nothing is impossible with him.

Offer Thanks: That a woman's body became the dwelling place of divinity.

Confess: Any tendency to devalue yourself as a woman.

Ask God: To make you a woman, like Mary, who brings Jesus into the world by expressing his character, power, forgiveness, and grace.

Lift Your Heart

Choose one episode in the life of Mary—her encounter with Gabriel, the birth of her child, the scene with the shepherds, the presentation in the temple, the Magi's visit, the escape to Egypt, her son's agony on the cross, or her presence with the disciples in the Upper Room. Imagine yourself in her place. What are your struggles, your joys? What thoughts run through your mind? Does anything or anyone take you by surprise?

Ask the Holy Spirit to guide your reflections, to help you imagine the sounds, sights, and smells that will bring each scene to life. Let the Scriptures feed your soul with a deeper understanding of God's intention for your life. Pray for the grace to be like the woman who said: "I am the Lord's servant. May it be to me as you have said."

My soul is full of you, my God, and I cannot hold back my gladness. Everyone who sees me will call me blessed because you have noticed me. You saw my lowliness and my need and filled my emptiness with your presence. Form your likeness in me so that, like Mary, I can bring you into a world that desperately needs your love. In the name of Mary's son I pray, Amen.

The Syrophoenician Woman

Her Character: Though a Gentile, she addressed Jesus as "Lord, Son of David." Her great faith resulted in her daughter's deliverance.

Her Sorrow: That her child was possessed by an evil spirit.

Her Joy: That Jesus freed her daughter from spiritual bondage.

Key Scriptures: Matthew 15:21–28; Mark 7:24–30

Her Story

Her body jerked and twisted, arms thrashing the air. Wide-eyed, the little girl spoke to ghosts her mother could not see, her face changing as rapidly as clouds in a sudden storm. Fear, surprise, and then a crazy kind of laughter, as though someone had stolen her soul. Dark hair stuck in gummy strands against her cheeks.

Her mother wondered what had become of the sweet child who had followed her like a puppy wherever she went. How she missed those soft kisses and the button nose that had nuzzled her cheek. She had hardly slept these last few nights for fear of what her daughter might do to herself. Neither of them, she thought, could stand much more.

Just that morning she had caught wind of a Jewish healer who, friends said, had come to Tyre hoping for relief from the crowds that mobbed him in Galilee. It didn't matter that Jews seldom mingled with Gentiles. She would go to him, beg his help, throw a fit herself if necessary. She would do whatever it took to get him to listen. It didn't take long to find him.

She approached Jesus, pleading, "Lord, Son of David, have mercy on me! My daughter is suffering terribly from demon-possession."

But Jesus ignored the woman, making no reply.

Finally, his disciples said to Jesus, "Send her away, for she keeps crying out after us."

But Jesus knew it would not be that easy to get rid of her. He told them, "I was sent only to the lost sheep of Israel."

Hearing him, the woman fell at his feet again, imploring, "Lord, help me!"

Then Jesus turned and said, "It is not right to take the children's bread and toss it to the dogs."

But the woman would not give up. "Yes, Lord," she said, "but even the dogs eat the crumbs that fall from their master's table."

"Woman, you have great faith! Your request is granted," Jesus said.

So the Syrophoenician woman returned to her daughter, who was delivered from the evil spirit the very same hour that Jesus had spoken.

Scripture doesn't describe the little girl of this story in any detail; it says only that she was possessed by a demon. But judging from similar incidents, such as that of the Gerasene demoniac, whose story is told in Luke 8, or the little boy in Matthew 17, who kept throwing himself in the fire, the signs of demonic possession were probably both obvious and frightening.

But why did Jesus seem so rude to the poor woman, ignoring her request and then referring to her and her child as dogs?

His response may sound a little less harsh when you realize that the word he used for "dogs" was not the derisive one Jews ordinarily reserved for Gentiles. Instead, it was the term used for little dogs kept as pets. Jesus was also making it clear that his primary mission was to the Israelites. Had Jesus performed healings and miracles in Tyre and Sidon, he would have risked the same kind of mob scenes he had just left behind in Galilee, thus inaugurating a ministry to the Gentiles in advance of his Father's timing.

The woman couldn't have known the reason for his silence, however, and it must have tested her faith. But rather than give up or take offense, she exercised her quick wit, revealing both a deep humility and tenacious faith. It was a combination Jesus seemed unable to resist—fertile soil in which to grow a miracle. The Syrophoenician woman must have rejoiced that day to see the daughter she loved safe and sane, grateful for the life-giving bread that had fallen from the Master's table.

Her Life and Times

Demon Possession

The New Testament teems with stories of people possessed by demons. Demons are fallen angels, emissaries of Satan, sent to earth to oppress human beings and lead them astray. Under Satan's control, their only goal is to further his purposes. They have supernatural powers here on earth: supernatural intelligence — they know and try to hide the truth (1 John 4:1–3) and they recognize Jesus as God's Son (Mark 5:7); and supernatural strength — a man possessed by demons could break away even when chained (Luke 8:29).

Though supernatural in their strength, demons are not more powerful than God or his Son. Whenever demons came face to face with Christ or his disciples in the New Testament, they trembled and did their bidding.

What the New Testament describes as demon-possessed people we would today depict as having an illness of some sort, physical or mental. How much distinction can be made between the two is uncertain. After Jesus cast a demon out of one man, he was described as "sitting there, dressed and in his right mind" (Mark 5:15). The man's demon possession could easily have been extreme mental illness. At times, demon possession caused muteness or blindness or convulsions (Matthew 9:32; 12:22; Mark 9:20). We can only speculate whether today we would view these illnesses as purely physical.

It is interesting to note that demons are mentioned only twice in the Old Testament (Deuteronomy 32:17; Psalm 106:37), yet over seventy times in the New Testament—all but a few of those in the Gospels. Perhaps Jesus' ministry to the sick exposed demonic activity as never before. Or perhaps Satan focused an extraordinary amount of his strength and power over the land of Israel while Jesus walked and healed there.

When Jesus left this earth, he sent the Holy Spirit to indwell his people. The life of Christ within us, as believers, is our defense against the forces of evil. We may suffer from physical, emotional, or mental illnesses that seem like demons within us, and God often uses the power of medical treatment to heal us of those illnesses—but let's not discount the power we possess within ourselves as children of God. That power forms a hedge of protection around and within us as we maintain a close relationship with God the Father, Christ his Son, and the Holy Spirit, our strength and comfort.

Her Legacy in Scripture

Read Matthew 15:21–22

1. What about these words makes it obvious that this woman and her daughter were both suffering?
2. If your child were the one possessed, how would you approach Jesus for healing? What would you say? How would you act?

Read Matthew 15:23

3. Why do you suppose Jesus at first ignored the woman? What was her response?
4. Was it okay for this woman to keep "crying out"? Why or why not?

Read Matthew 15:24–26

5. This woman was not an Israelite. What might have been her response to Jesus' statement that he had come "only to the lost sheep of Israel"? Why do you think she didn't give up?
6. How persistent are you in prayer? Do you give up easily? Or do you keep praying until you get a definite answer?

Read Matthew 15:27–28

7. What was meant by the "crumbs" in verse 27? What was this woman saying?

8. What was Jesus' response? Why did he respond in the way he did?
9. When have you asked for little and received much? Were you surprised? How often do we settle for the "crumbs" when Jesus really wants to give us the whole loaf?

Reread Matthew 15:23, 28

10. What is the difference between how the disciples responded to the woman and how Jesus ultimately responded to her?
11. When a needy person approaches you, do you respond like Jesus or like his disciples? How do you respond if the person is emotionally needy—continually sticking close to you, interrupting your conversations with others, asking questions you can't answer, and generally wanting more than you wish to give?

Her Promise

What possible promise can be found in a pagan woman whose little girl was possessed by an evil spirit? The Syrophoenician woman wouldn't have known what to do about her daughter had she not heard about Jesus. Somehow, she was given the faith to believe that he was the only one capable of saving her child.

Evil spirits, unfortunately, are not creatures of a former age. We too must fight the evil powers in own lives. The difference now is that Jesus has won the ultimate victory on the cross. As believers, we share in his victory. He has given us authority over the evil forces in our lives. We may still be fighting the battle, but, absurd as it sounds, the victory is already won!

Promises in Scripture

Finally, be strong in the Lord and in his mighty power.
—Ephesians 6:10

Every spirit that acknowledges that Jesus Christ has come in the flesh is from God, but every spirit that does not acknowledge Jesus is not from God.

—1 John 4:2–3

The one who is in you is greater than the one who is in the world.

—1 John 4:4

Her Legacy of Prayer

Then Jesus answered, "Woman, you have great faith! Your request is granted."

—Matthew 15:28

Reflect On: Matthew 15:21 – 28.

Praise God: For his power to deliver us from every form of evil.

Offer Thanks: For the deliverance you have already experienced.

Confess: Any hopelessness about your children or others you love.

Ask God: To give you the same "terrier-like" faith that the Syrophoenician woman had, so that you will never give up praying for the salvation of your loved ones.

Lift Your Heart

Though most of our children will never suffer from actual demonic possession, all of them are engaged, as we are, in a spiritual battle. As a mother, your prayers and your life play a role in the spiritual protection of your children. This week, pray Psalm 46 or Psalm 91 for the spiritual protection of your family. Or take a few moments to pray these verses from Psalm 125:

> *Those who trust in the LORD are like Mount Zion,*
>   *which cannot be shaken but endures forever.*
> *As the mountains surround Jerusalem,*
>   *so the LORD surrounds his people*
>   *both now and forevermore.*

Imagine that every member of your family is surrounded by God, just as mountains surround the city of Jerusalem. Offer each one to him, placing them in his care. When you are worried about a particular family member, pray a quick prayer asking God to surround him or her with his protection.

Lord, surround my children like the mountains surrounding Jerusalem. Encircle our family with your power and peace. Deliver us from evil now and forever. Amen.

Salome, Mother of the Sons of Zebedee

Her Name Means *Peace*

Her Character:	A devoted follower of Jesus, whose husband ran a fishing business, she shared the common misconception that the Messiah would drive out the Romans and establish a literal kingdom in Palestine. Her name was probably Salome.
Her Sorrow:	To have stood with other women at the cross, witnessing the death of Jesus of Nazareth.
Her Joy:	To have seen an angel at Christ's tomb, who proclaimed the resurrection.
Key Scriptures:	Matthew 20:20–24; 27:56; Mark 15:40–41; 16:1–2

Her Story

Salome loved Jesus nearly as much as she loved her own two sons, James and John. She would never forget the day they had left their father and their fishing nets to follow him. Lately, she too had come to believe that Jesus was the Messiah of God.

She had smiled when she heard Jesus had nicknamed her boys "the Sons of Thunder." Surely he had recognized the seeds of greatness in the two feisty brothers from Capernaum. Why else would he have invited them into his inner circle, along with Simon Peter? She had heard how Jesus had led the three up a high mountain. When they came down, her garrulous sons could hardly speak. But then the story came out.

"Jesus' face was blindingly bright like the sun....

"Moses and Elijah appeared and spoke with him....

"Suddenly a cloud surrounded us and a voice from heaven said, 'This is my Son, whom I love; with him I am well pleased. Listen to him!'"

Salome had listened. She had seen the glory and the power that radiated from the man. Though she had heard ominous rumors that Jerusalem's men of power hated Jesus, she also knew that the great King David had faced his own share of enemies before establishing his kingdom. And hadn't Jesus promised his disciples that they would sit on twelve thrones in his kingdom? "Everyone who has left houses or brothers or sisters or father or mother or children or fields for my sake," he had said, "will receive a hundred times as much and will inherit eternal life." How could she doubt him? Even with faith small as a mustard seed, mountains could be moved.

Salome had left behind her comfortable home on the northwest shore of Galilee to join her sons. Now, as they journeyed up to Jerusalem, she remembered other words Jesus had spoken: "Ask and it will be given to you; seek and you will find; knock and the door will be opened to you." She would no longer deny herself the one favor her heart desired. Prostrating herself before him, she begged, "Grant that one of these two sons of mine may sit at your right and the other at your left in your kingdom."

But instead of replying to her, Jesus turned to James and John and said, "You don't know what you are asking. Can you drink the cup I am going to drink?"

"We can," they answered.

Jesus said to them, "You will indeed drink from my cup, but to sit at my right or left is not for me to grant. These places belong to those for whom they have been prepared by my Father."

Jesus, who knew Zebedee's sons better than anyone, realized that Salome was only voicing their rising ambitions. Like any loving mother, she had simply asked for what she thought would make her children happy. But as Jesus' reply and subsequent events proved, this mother didn't begin to comprehend what she was asking. Soon, the man she had approached as a king would himself die on a cross, and she would be one of the women who witnessed his death.

After it was over, Salome may have remembered the anguished faces of the men who had been crucified with Jesus, one on his right hand and the other on his left—an ironic reminder of her request on the way up to Jerusalem. Such a memory would only have increased her terror for what might now happen to her sons.

Along with other faithful women at the cross, Salome was present on the morning of Jesus' resurrection. Surely the angel's words — "He has risen! He is not here!" — would have comforted her later in life when her son James became the first martyred apostle, dying at the hands of Herod Agrippa.

Instead of asking Jesus what he wanted for her sons, Salome acted as though she knew exactly what he needed to do on their behalf. She must have forgotten that Jesus had exhorted his followers to leave behind not only houses, brothers and sisters, fathers and mothers for his sake, but also children. In Salome's case, it didn't mean turning her back on her children but surrendering them to God. It meant putting Jesus above everything and everyone, loving him better than her own sons. Only then would she understand the meaning of what they would suffer as followers of Christ. Only then would she really know how to pray.

Her Life and Times

Mothering

In biblical times, when a man married, he gained another possession. Every wife was under her husband's absolute authority. When a man decided "to marry a wife," the meaning of the phrase was closer to "become the master of a wife." But even though a woman's position in the household was one of subservience to her husband, she was still in a higher position than anyone else in the household.

A woman's principal duty was to produce a family, preferably sons, who could ensure the family's physical and financial future. Mothers generally nursed their youngsters until they were about three years old. During that time, husbands and wives did not usually engage in sexual intercourse, a natural form of birth control that gave the mother time to devote herself to her youngest child.

Mothers had total care of their children, both sons and daughters, until they were about six years old. The children helped their mother with household tasks, and she taught them basic lessons on living in their culture. After six years of age, most boys became the family shepherd or began to spend the day with their father, learning the family business. David, as the youngest son, took care of his family's sheep and goats (1 Samuel 16:11), and Jesus probably spent time with his father Joseph learning his carpentry trade (Mark 6:3). Daughters stayed with their mothers throughout their growing-up years. Mothers taught them spinning and weaving and cooking, as well as how to behave and what to expect in their future roles as wives and mothers.

Gradually the role of mothers came to include activities like those described in Proverbs 31. Throughout Scripture, the role of mothering is given dignity and significance, so much so that God describes his love for us as his children in terms of mothering. "As a mother comforts her child, so will I [the Lord] comfort you" (Isaiah 66:13). Paul describes his care for the Thessalonians as the care of a mother for her children: "We were gentle among you, like a mother caring for her little children" (1 Thessalonians 2:7).

When you find yourself lost in the chaos and clutter of caring for young children, remember the important part you play in keeping their world safe and happy. When you find yourself buried in the mess and muddle of raising elementary school children, remember how much they rely on you for their security. When you find yourself struggling with the disaster and disarray of raising teenagers, remember how much you love them and how much they need you to believe in them. Never forget: If you have children, they are one of your greatest legacies.

Her Legacy in Scripture

Read Matthew 20:20–21

1. What did James's and John's mother really want? Do you think she was asking only for honor for her sons, or did she also want something for herself?
2. How do you react when your child is honored? How do you react when your child is passed over for some honor? How are you like Salome?

Read Matthew 20:22–23

3. What "cup" is Jesus talking about here? Do you think the disciples answered his question glibly or seriously?
4. Would it be wise to prevent all suffering in the lives of your children? Why or why not?

Read Matthew 20:24

5. Why were the other disciples upset with James and John instead of with James's and John's mother? Do you think James and John had some part in their mother's actions?
6. If you had been there, what would you have said to Salome? Have you ever said something similar to the mother of one of your child's friends, perhaps not to her face but at least to yourself? Why are mothers so eager to protect and elevate their own children?

Read Matthew 20:25–27

7. With these words, Jesus totally overturns the natural reactions of his culture and ours. How do you think the disciples and Salome reacted to his words? What do you think Salome may have been thinking at this point?

8. How easy or hard is it for you to play the role of servant? Define servant leadership. What has to change in your life for you to truly become a servant leader?

THURSDAY

Her Promise

Though the typical woman in biblical times was in a subservient role, her position as a mother is exalted by Scripture. God the Father recognized from the very beginning the important role a mother would play in her children's lives, and he promised to bless her. Those same promises apply to you today.

Promises in Scripture

God also said to Abraham, "As for Sarai your wife, you are no longer to call her Sarai; her name will be Sarah. I will bless her and will surely give you a son by her. I will bless her so that she will be the mother of nations; kings of peoples will come from her."

—Genesis 17:15–16

He settles the barren woman in her home
  as a happy mother of children.

—Psalm 113:9

Her children arise and call her blessed;
  her husband also, and he praises her:
"Many women do noble things,
  but you surpass them all."

—Proverbs 31:28–29

Can a mother forget the baby at her breast
  and have no compassion on the child she has borne?

—Isaiah 49:15

Her Legacy of Prayer

"Grant that one of these two sons of mine may sit at your right and the other at your left in your kingdom."

—Matthew 20:21

Reflect On: Matthew 20:20–28.

Praise God: That his Son has shown us the true meaning of greatness.

Offer Thanks: For all the ways, large and small, that God has served you.

Confess: Pride and misguided ambition.

Ask God: For the grace to make the connection that the way down leads to the way up, that it is the humble woman who will be considered great in the kingdom.

Lift Your Heart

Many women have heard the message of servanthood and internalized it in unhealthy ways. Instead of realizing their inherent dignity as women, they have defined their worth primarily in terms of others. But both men and women are called to model themselves on Christ, who was not a person who suffered from low self-esteem. His humility wasn't a cover for a sense of unworthiness.

If you have made the mistake of living your life through your husband or your children, ask God for the grace to change. Admit you are a human being who needs care, consideration, and replenishment. Ask God to restore balance in your life. But as you go through the process of finding balance, don't eliminate the word "humility" from your vocabulary by embracing a life of selfishness. This week, ask each day for eyes to see another's need. Then ask for grace to serve in a way that truly models the humility of Jesus.

Lord, forgive me for any pride that has crowded you out of my heart. Whenever I am tempted to think or act with selfish ambition, place a check in my spirit. Give me, instead, the courage to be a servant. Make more room in my heart for your love, I pray.